CAN YOU DIG IT?

❋ What was the Weather Bureau? (See page 3.)

❋ Who was the eighth member of the Chicago Seven? (See page 9.)

❋ In what year did Roger Maris hit 61 home runs? (See page 91.)

❋ Who was the first black student to enroll at Ole Miss? (See page 37.)

❋ What 1960s celebrity described himself as "an erotic politician"? (See page 40.)

❋ Who was Barbie's best friend? (See page 106.)

❋ What ever happened to Baby Jane? (See page 85.)

❋ How many babies were born at Woodstock? (See page 50.)

❋ What was the Supremes' first hit? (See page 45.)

❋ Who referred to marriage as "legalized rape"? (See page 29.)

❋ Who invented the topless bathing suit? (See page 107.)

It happened...

Only Yesterday

GW00693567

Only Yesterday

A Quiz on the Sixties

Paul Cowan

WARNER BOOKS

A Warner Communications Company

Warner Books, Inc., 666 Fifth Avenue, New York, NY 10103
W A Warner Communications Company

Printed in the United States Of America
First printing: January 1990
10 9 8 7 6 5 4 3 2 1

Library of Congress Cataloging-in-Publication Data
Cowan, Paul.
    Only yesterday: a quiz on the sixties / Paul Cowan.
        p.   cm.
    ISBN 0-446-39036-4
    1. United States—History—1961–1969—Miscellanea. 2. United States—
Civilization—1945—Miscellanea. 3. Questions and answers. I. Title.
E841.C64   1990
973.92—dc20   89-16723
                                                          CIP

BOOK DESIGN BY GIORGETTA BELL MCREE
COVER DESIGN BY SEYMOUR CHWAST

Acknowledgments

Paul Cowan's family and friends worked to complete this book after his death last fall. Graham Boynton, Todd Gitlin, Laura K. Handman, David Horowitz, Mark Jacobson, Robert Krulwich, Jack Newfield, Linda Perney, Ruth Rosen, Gabriel Ross, and Jean Strouse all contributed questions and answers to the quiz. Linda Perney edited it. Many thanks to all of them.

Contents

Preface

When I was a boy, my parents displayed Frederick Lewis Allen's *Only Yesterday* in the book-lined room they called the library. For them, the evocative picture and text brought back the honeyed, difficult years of their youth. I felt an almost magnetic attraction to the book. For me, it re-created an America I had never known—an America I nonetheless somehow felt I had inhabited.

I hope my *Only Yesterday*—this quiz book—does for readers what Allen's book did for my parents and me. For people in their thirties, forties, and fifties, the questions are intended to make the past that feels like it was just a week or two ago tangible to people who may have forgotten the details that made a first love, a first political passion, an intellectual discovery so exciting. A song lyric, an image from a movie, a sports event, a memory of fashion or politics can reopen the doors of rich youthful experience. These memories restore dimension to life.

These same questions are intended to suggest the richness and texture of the sixties to younger people who have read and heard about the decade, but still feel outside it. Recently there have been some wonderful works that brought the past alive: movies like *The Big Chill*, TV documentaries like *Eyes on the Prize*, and TV shows like *The Wonder Years*. I hope that, in its way, *Only Yesterday* will serve the same function.

I've asked a lot of questions about music since music is a living bridge across the generations. And I've looked at movies, since young people tend to know the sixties through VCRs. I've also asked about conventional politics, New Left politics, the civil rights movement, theater, fashion, and sports. To create a sense of play, I've suggested some wacky answers to my questions—answers that mix up categories, people, and events wildly. If it's not the correct answer, it didn't happen, no matter how plausible a possibility may sound. And some questions have more than one correct answer. I hope people don't score themselves on the quiz, since it is supposed to be for fun, not competition.

I hope this is as much fun for you to do as it was for me to write.

Introduction

Paul Cowan was a participant in and a product of the state of mind we call "the sixties." He was in Mississippi, SDS, the Peace Corps, the anti-war movement, and outside the Chicago convention of 1968. He was an anarchic spirit, a rebel against illegitimate authority, an agent of change—in short, he was part of the zeitgeist.

But his part of it was more in the loving, whimsical style of the Beatles than in the raunchy decadence of the Rolling Stones; more in the nonviolent, communitarian style of Dr. Martin Luther King, Jr., than the ego-tripping of Timothy Leary or Jerry Rubin.

Paul and I met in 1964 and we shared most of the same sixties tastes. We admired Orwell, Agee, Camus, Bob Moses, Phil Ochs, Sandy Koufax, Joan Baez, Muhammad Ali, Norman Mailer, and Motown music. He had a wonderful sense of the varieties and absurdities of the sixties experience. He knew all about mass culture, baseball, food, religion, rock 'n' roll. He was an enthusiast.

In 1967 he wrote a book called *The Making of an Un-American.* It was a very sixties sort of title, but I think the internationalist intent might have been misunderstood by some. Paul was as American as a hot dog at a July 4 doubleheader.

That's what made him such an extraordinary journalist. Paul liked the average American at a time when the New Left was alienated from the patriotic, beer-drinking working class.

Paul got his best stories in pure American places like tenements on the Lower East Side of New York, black churches in the rural

South, and at George Wallace rallies in the industrial cities of Massachusetts. He had a great ear. He could hear America singing; he could listen to the invisible man.

Paul worked on this book during the year he was dying of leukemia. It kept his mind off his blood and it kept his memory engaged in a season he enjoyed. What I said at Paul's funeral still stands: "Paul was the best of us. He was the bravest, the gentlest, the purest of our gang. He taught us how to live. And he taught us how to die."

JACK NEWFIELD
January, 1989

THE QUESTIONS

Politics and News

1. James Forman was:
a. the 1964 Olympic heavyweight championship winner
b. the executive secretary of the Congress of Racial Equality
c. a Czech film director
d. the executive director of the Student Nonviolent Coordinating Committee

2. What was the Weather Bureau?
a. a rock-jazz fusion group
b. the name of the Weatherpeople leadership at the 1968 SDS convention
c. the name of the Weather Underground magazine
d. Bob Dylan's first backup band

3. Who wrote Barry Goldwater's acceptance speech at the 1964 Republican convention? What happened to him?
a. William Safire wrote the speech. He later worked for Richard Nixon.
b. Ed Meese wrote the speech. He later worked for Ronald Reagan.
c. David Horowitz and Peter Collier wrote the speech. Formerly committed leftists, they had come to embrace the right wing.
d. Karl Hess III wrote the speech. A militant right-winger, he later became a radical leftist.

4. Suppose you were a demonstrator at the 1968 Democratic Convention in Chicago, or during the Days of Rage or Stop the Draft Week in New York. What movie spurred you on?
a. *Joe*
b. *The Battle of Algiers*
c. *Wild in the Streets*
d. *Alice's Restaurant*

5. What crimes were Father Philip Berrigan and Sister Elizabeth McAlister indicted for (and subsequently acquitted)?
a. They were accused of pouring blood on Pennsylvania draft records.
b. They were accused of conspiring to contaminate the water supply of Washington, D.C., with LSD.
c. They were accused of conspiring to kidnap Henry Kissinger and blow up the steam pipes beneath Washington, D.C.
d. They were accused of conspiring to bomb the New York City headquarters of Dow Chemical.

6. What was the Walker Report? What happened to Walker?
a. It was a report on violence at the 1968 Democratic convention; Walker later became governor of Illinois.
b. It was a report on violence in the inner city; Walker became a Supreme Court justice.
c. It was the official report on the assassination of JFK. Walker became the president of the University of Chicago.
d. It was the classified report on the conduct of the Vietnam War that *The New York Times* later printed as the Pentagon Papers. Walker was later tried for leaking the report.

7. Mario Savio was:
a. the first Italian to win at Wimbledon
b. the founder of Berkeley's Free Speech Movement
c. the author of the poem "Bread and Roses"
d. an ex-cop Congressman from the Bronx

8. Malcolm X was shot in
a. the Abyssinian Baptist Church
b. the Apollo Theater
c. the Audubon Ballroom
d. the Cotton Club

4

9. When Lyndon Johnson stepped into the well of the House of Representatives and announced "We shall overcome," he was:
a. exhorting the American military to win the war in Vietnam
b. lobbying for passage of the Voting Rights Act
c. announcing the War on Poverty
d. predicting the outcome of his forthcoming gall-bladder operation

10. Allard Lowenstein:
a. was the head of the New York City chapter of the United Federation of Teachers and led the teachers' strike
b. implied that the leaders of the 1968 Chicago protests were Communists
c. started the "Dump Johnson" movement that sparkplugged Eugene McCarthy's presidential campaign
d. told Robert Kennedy he'd support Kennedy if he were made Secretary of Education

11. One of the defendants at the 1968 Chicago conspiracy trial was gagged and handcuffed to a chair for days. His/her name was:
a. Abbie Hoffman
b. Huey P. Newton
c. Bobby Seale
d. Bernardine Dohrn

12. The Port Huron Statement was:
a. a landmark trade agreement between Canada and the U.S.
b. a seminal document about the New Left
c. an agreement between England's Labour and Liberal parties that enabled Harold Wilson to become Prime Minister
d. the manifesto that Allen Ginsberg, Gregory Corso, and Gary Snyder wrote proclaiming the Beat Generation

13. "If you aren't part of the solution you're part of the problem." These are the words of:
a. Andy Warhol
b. Daniel Cohn-Bendit
c. Eugene McCarthy
d. Eldridge Cleaver

14. Who called Sirhan Sirhan a Yippie?
a. Abbie Hoffman
b. King Hussein

c. Stokely Carmichael
d. Jerry Rubin

15. Who was James Chaney?
a. one of the three civil-rights workers murdered in Mississippi during the Freedom Summer
b. a leader of Chicago's Blackstone Rangers
c. the Black Panther minister of defense
d. the first student to attempt to integrate a Woolworth's lunch counter

16. Viola Liuzzo was:
a. Carlo Gambino's mistress
b. the first Italian woman to win at Forest Hills
c. a Detroit housewife shot while driving a demonstrator home from the Selma march
d. the lead singer for the Mamas and the Papas

17. Whose Justice Department prosecuted Dr. Benjamin Spock?
a. John Mitchell
b. Ramsey Clark
c. Robert Morgenthau
d. Guy Goodwin

18. Inside the Chicago Amphitheater, on the third night of the 1968 Democratic Convention, Connecticut Senator Abraham Ribicoff took the podium to denounce "gestapo tactics" in the streets of Chicago. Although Mayor Daley later denied it, some TV viewers claimed that Daley muttered:
a. "You're right, we can't all be Eichmanns. I'll muzzle the police."
b. "You're right. But if we nominate Hubert Humphrey and win the election, all this will be forgotten."
c. "You Jew son of a bitch."
d. "Shut up, you son of a bitch, or Connecticut won't ever get a sewer system when Humphrey becomes President."

19. In October 1969, the Weatherman faction of SDS battled police during the revolutionary action they called The Days of Rage. At their December National War Council in Flint, Michigan, they designed a new radical symbol—and showed their revolutionary zeal by thrusting four fingers in the air. The weathermen were:

a. lashing back at their rich parents who would rather say "fore" on a golf course than help the poor
b. reminding each other that they were the vanguard of the fourth-world revolutionary movement
c. giving the "fork salute," which showed their solidarity with Charles Manson and his group, who had killed actress Sharon Tate and thrust a fork in her stomach.
d. symbolically recreating an initiation rite—they had to kill four cops to become part of the Weather elite

20. When Abbie Hoffman and his Yippie friends went to Wall Street in the sixties, he:
a. organized a be-in so that stockbrokers could show their opposition to the war in Vietnam
b. tried to levitate the Dow
c. applied for a job as an investment broker so he could help finance the revolution
d. tore up dollar bills to show contempt for the capitalist system

21. When Jerry Rubin went to Wall Street in the eighties, he:
a. organized a be-in so that stockbrokers could show their opposition to American support for the Nicaraguan contras
b. tried to levitate the Dow
c. applied for a job as an investment broker so that he could enjoy a more pleasant lifestyle
d. glued pieces of dollar bills together to show that the sixties have reconciled with the eighties

22. During the 1968 Democratic Convention the Yippies chose for their presidential candidate:
a. John Lennon
b. a pig named Pigasus
c. Eldridge Cleaver
d. a donkey named Fred

23. The judge who presided over the 1968 Chicago Conspiracy Trial was:
a. David Horowitz
b. Julius J. Hoffman
c. Julius Lester
d. Irving Kaufman

24. Marjorie Michelmore was:

a. Marjorie Morningstar's name before she became an actress

b. an early performance artist who played cello bare-breasted

c. a Peace Corps volunteer who dropped a postcard that offended her Nigerian hosts when they read it

d. an ex-nun who poured blood on draft cards in Catonsville, Maryland

25. The Stonewall Uprising happened:

a. after Harvey Milk was assassinated in San Francisco

b. after Anita Bryant announced her campaign against gays in Dade County

c. after New York City police raided a gay bar in Sheridan Square in Greenwich Village

d. after the Supreme Court upheld a Georgia statute outlawing homosexual relations between consenting adults

26. That was the same night that:

a. Malcolm X was assassinated

b. RFK was assassinated

c. Dr. Martin Luther King, Jr., was assassinated

d. Judy Garland's wake was held

27. Who said, "I am skeptical of the ability of black revolutionaries to achieve a fair trial anywhere in the United States"?

a. Huey P. Newton of the Black Panther Party

b. William Kunstler, lawyer for the Chicago Seven

c. Kingman Brewster, President of Yale University

d. Ramsey Clark, former Attorney General

28. Who said, "the only...position for women...is prone"?

a. Stokely Carmichael

b. H. Rap Brown

c. Norman Mailer

d. Joe Namath

29. The remark was made:

a. during a radio phone-in show, when a caller claimed to have seen women leading the looting of a furniture store. The remark was meant to refute the caller.

b. on *The Dick Cavett Show* as a defense of the argument in *Prisoner of Sex*

c. to two female civil-rights workers after they protested that most women in the movement were undervalued

d. to a *Village Voice* reporter as a sign of masculinity

30. The teach-in movement was:

a. an attempt to boost the grades of college students who were afraid they'd lose their draft deferments if they flunked their courses

b. a student protest ignited at Berkeley which was designed to make college curricula more relevant

c. a nationwide movement designed to teach the pros and cons of the war in Vietnam

d. a Johnson administration effort to convince college graduates to join VISTA as teachers

31. If you rode the subways in the mid-sixties in New York City, you were sure to see a poster with the slogan "He's fresh and everyone else is tired." Who was he?

a. John V. Lindsay, symbol of the new politician

b. Willis Reed, symbol of the new athlete

c. Tom Wolfe, symbol of the new journalism

d. a Green Beret, symbol of the new army

32. Operation Abolition was:

a. the name Dr. Martin Luther King, Jr., gave to the national voter registration drive his organization launched

b. a government-sponsored program to spray paraquat on marijuana patches grown in Mexico

c. a film released by the government with footage of the demonstrations against the House Un-American Activities Committee hearings in San Francisco

d. an SDS campaign to lobby senators to abolish the draft

33. Who was the eighth member of the Chicago Seven?

a. Fred Hampton

b. Mark Rudd

c. Huey P. Newton

d. Bobby Seale

34. What was the name of the commune that considered expelling Tom Hayden?

a. the Total Loss Farm
b. the Diggers
c. the Red Family
d. the Hog Farm

35. What Republican did *not* campaign for the presidency in the 1968 primary season?
a. Nelson Rockefeller
b. George Romney
c. John V. Lindsay
d. Richard Nixon

36. Who was Abe Zapruder? Why did he become famous?
a. He was one of Hollywood's early independent filmmakers and was well known for his opposition to the blacklist in the fifties.
b. He was an investment banker on Wall Street during the go-go years; his innovative approach to international finance laid the groundwork for the bull market of the eighties.
c. He was the managing editor of *The New York Times*
d. He was a Dallas-based dress manufacturer who shot footage of JFK's assassination on his home movie camera.

37. Who said: "I've had women's lib up to here"?
a. Joe Namath
b. Hugh Hefner
c. Strom Thurmond
d. Dr. Edgar F. Berman, a Democratic Party activist/physician

38. A political miracle took place "in the snows of New Hampshire" —the New Hampshire primary of 1968. The majority of delegates were won by:
a. Lyndon Johnson
b. Hubert Humphrey
c. Eugene McCarthy
d. Robert Kennedy

39. Who said, "Violence is as American as cherry pie"?
a. Sam Peckinpah
b. The Underground Gourmet
c. *Village Voice* rock critic Richard Goldstein
d. H. Rap Brown

40. The fifty-mile hike—originally an endurance test for marine recruits—became a craze among New Frontiersmen. Which staffer backed out after publicly promising to complete one?
a. Edward R. Murrow
b. Pierre Salinger
c. Ted Sorensen
d. Newton Minow

41. Dr. Martin Luther King, Jr.'s, chief lieutenant was:
a. Rev. Andrew Young
b. Rev. Jesse Jackson
c. Rev. Ralph D. Abernathy
d. Medgar Evers

42. Which of the following sixties radical leaders did not experience a religious conversion in the seventies and eighties?
a. H. Rap Brown
b. Eldridge Cleaver
c. Julius Lester
d. Abbie Hoffman

43. What sixties activist lost credibility by saying that he/she had been brainwashed about Vietnam?
a. Jane Fonda
b. Daniel Ellsberg
c. Prisoner of war Jeremiah Denton
d. George Romney

44. Which of the following politicians was *not* one of Dr. Martin Luther King, Jr.'s, assistants in the Southern Christian Leadership Conference (SCLC)?
a. Jesse Jackson, presidential candidate
b. Richard Arrington, mayor of Birmingham, Alabama
c. Walter Fauntroy, representative from Washington, D.C.
d. Andrew Young, mayor of Atlanta

45. Which of the following politicians did *not* get his start as an activist for SNCC?
a. Ron Dellums, congressman from Oakland, California
b. John Lewis, congressman from Atlanta, Georgia
c. Marion Barry, mayor of Washington, D.C.
d. Julian Bond, state assemblyman, Atlanta, Georgia

46. Kenneth Keating was a respected senator from New York. During his campaign against Robert F. Kennedy, he:

a. debated an empty chair, which symbolized Keating's charge that Kennedy was a "carpetbagger"
b. attacked the Kennedy brothers' record on civil rights
c. attacked RFK for once having worked on Senator Joe McCarthy's staff
d. attacked the Kennedy brothers for their handling of the Cuban missile crisis, calling it immature

47. Operation Phoenix was:

a. a CIA-supported program to identify and neutralize Vietcong leaders
b. Dr. Christiaan Barnard's name for his first successful heart transplant
c. a popular song sung by Glen Campbell
d. a Republican drive to register voters in the Sun Belt

48. Redstockings was:

a. a look designed by Mary Quant
b. the first team to play women's professional baseball
c. an organization of filmmakers called up in front of the House Un-American Activities Committee
d. an early feminist group

49. If you sought out Owsley in 1967, you were:

a. in Danang, looking for the Vietnam War's equivalent of Kilroy
b. trying to emulate the hero of *V*
c. trying out a new brand of children's aspirin
d. in San Francisco, looking to score exotic drugs

50. Who coined the phrase "limousine liberal"?

a. Mario Procaccino
b. Phil Ochs
c. Spiro Agnew
d. Tom Wolfe

51. What or who was Big O?

a. the apocalyptic orgasm
b. Odetta
c. Jackie Onassis
d. Ondine's

52. In 1968, Chicago's Blackstone Rangers:
a. sent their two star players to their National Hockey League affiliate, the New York Rangers
b. recorded their hit single "You Teased Me Too Often"
c. received federal poverty funding
d. become famous then they captured Hill 92 from the Vietcong

53. Who worried publicly about losing his "precious bodily fluids"?
a. General Jack D. Ripper in *Dr. Strangelove*
b. Doors lead singer Jim Morrison
c. John Birch Society founder Robert Welch
d. the therapist Arthur Ganor

54. Who shot Andy Warhol?
a. Squeaky Fromme
b. Valerie Solanis
c. Susan Atkins
d. Viva

55. Bernadette Devlin was:
a. a leader of the Weather Underground
b. a former nun who, along with several others, poured duck's blood on draft files
c. a supporter of the IRA who was elected to the House of Commons
d. an early, outspoken right-to-lifer

56. Annie Glenn refused to let Vice President Johnson into her house before her husband, John Glenn, was launched into space. She was:
a. an ardent opponent of the war in Vietnam
b. afraid she would stutter
c. so afraid for her husband's safety that she couldn't cope with a stranger
d. afraid to violate an exclusive rights agreement she had made with *Life* magazine

57. "I am prepared to wait until hell freezes over" was said at a time of heightened international tensions. Who said it, where did he say it, and during what crisis?
a. JFK said it during his Vienna summit meeting with Khrushchev, while he was waiting for Khrushchev to answer his question

about whether or not the Soviets would dismantle the Berlin Wall.

b. Fidel Castro said it during the Cuban Missile Crisis on a telephone hookup to the United Nations Security Council.

c. G. Gordon Liddy said it during the Bay of Pigs invasion, while he waited for White House confirmation of a rumor that U.S. troops would be permitted to land as support for the landing force on the beaches.

d. Adlai Stevenson said it during a Security Council session during the Cuban Missile Crisis.

58. In July 1968, Gloria Steinem was:
a. planning to burn bras at the 1968 Miss America pageant.
b. a political reporter for *New York* magazine
c. a Playboy bunny
d. a graduate student writing her Ph.D. thesis on Betty Friedan

59. The embodiment of Jewish self-confidence in 1967 was:
a. Elie Wiesel
b. Barbra Streisand
c. Moshe Dayan
d. Mark Spitz

60. They called Lyndon Johnson "Landslide Lyndon" because he:
a. routed Barry Goldwater in 1964
b. won his first congressional election by a narrow margin
c. rescued his daughter Luci from an earthslide on a camping trip in the Grand Tetons
d. was so adept with Jewish voters that the Yiddish-speaking ones called him "Landsleit Lyndon"

61. Who supported the Days of Rage?
a. Bernadette Devlin
b. Bernadette Peters
c. Bernardine Dohrn
d. Bernie Cornfeld

62. "Ich bin ein _____."
a. German
b. Berliner
c. Viennese
d. Hamburger

63. In 1969, a townhouse on New York City's fashionable West 10th Street was blown up by radicals who were using it as a bomb factory. How much was the house said to be worth at that time?
a. $100,000
b. $250,000
c. $500,000
d. $1,000,000

64. "Burn, baby, burn" was:
a. the chant feminists in Atlantic City used as they burned their bras
b. the last words American GIs said as they left My Lai
c. the chant that became common during the urban riots of the sixties
d. the chant the devil used in an ad for a highly popular suntan lotion

65. Braniff stewardesses gained notoriety because:
a. They all had Texas accents.
b. They wore varicolored miniskirts.
c. They invented the Mile High Club.
d. They sang backup for the Jefferson Airplane.

66. Which feminist star was the first to come out in support of Berkeley's free speech movement?
a. Jane Fonda
b. Shirley MacLaine
c. Joan Baez
d. Jean Seberg

67. Match the quote and the politician:
a. "We seek no wider war."
b. "We will never fear to negotiate, but we will never negotiate out of fear."
c. "nattering nabobs of negativism."
d. "bring us together."

1. Spiro Agnew
2. Richard Nixon
3. Lyndon Johnson
4. John F. Kennedy

68. Who was the first director of the Peace Corps?
a. Sargent Shriver

b. Sam Brown

c. Theodore Sorensen

d. Richard Goodwin

69. "Now the trumpet summons us again." This phrase is from:

a. Dr. Martin Luther King, Jr.'s, speech at the March on Washington

b. John F. Kennedy's Inaugural Address

c. Lyndon Johnson's 1965 announcement of the first major troop increase in Vietnam

d. Louis Armstrong's introduction of Bob Dylan at the Newport Jazz Festival

70. On Sunday, March 7, 1965, civil rights workers marching in Selma, Alabama, were attacked by police. The place where they were beaten became a national symbol, just as the beating itself spurred passage of the Voting Rights Act. Where were they when they were beaten?

a. the Edmund Pettus Bridge

b. Neshoba County

c. the Tallahatchie Bridge

d. the Selma branch of Woolworth's

71. After Ché Guevara was killed, American magazines bid ferociously for his diary. Which one published it?

a. *Life*

b. *The Village Voice*

c. *Ramparts*

d. *The New York Times*

72. John F. Kennedy quoted the Chinese proverb "success has a thousand fathers; failure is an orphan" after:

a. the death of his son Patrick

b. his victory in the West Virginia primary

c. his brother's decision to run in New York

d. the Bay of Pigs

73. Camelot came to characterize the Kennedy White House:

a. because John Kennedy hosted Cabinet meetings at a large round table

b. in a joking pun made by Pierre Salinger, characterizing the sex lives of the White House staff

c. after President Kennedy was assassinated, when Jacqueline

Kennedy said that her husband had played the album from the show *Camelot* as he fell asleep every night

d. after President Kennedy made a breakthrough toward peace with his call for a test ban treaty.

74. Who accused Herbert Lehman, former governor of New York, of bossism?
a. Ed Koch
b. Robert Kennedy
c. Carmine De Sapio
d. Thomas Dewey

75. John F. Kennedy said, "Maybe this is the night I should go to the theater." He said it after:
a. he neutralized the segregationists at the University of Mississippi by sending in the Border Patrol
b. he threatened to nationalize the steel industry
c. he created a strike force to investigate the Mafia
d. the Cuban missile crisis

76. What was the Maddox?
a. the restaurant owned by Georgia Governor Lester Maddox
b. the gift shop owned by Georgia Governor Lester Maddox
c. one of two U.S. destroyers that figured in the Tonkin Gulf incident
d. the name of the ship seized by the North Koreans

77. When Dr. Martin Luther King, Jr., decided to bring the civil rights movement north, he:
a. organized a stall-in on the opening day of the 1964 New York World's Fair
b. launched the 1966 drive for fair housing in Chicago
c. lobbied and demonstrated for the desegregation of Boston schools in 1965
d. rang doorbells for Kenneth Gibson, Carl Stokes, and Richard Hatcher, black candidates for mayor in Newark, Cleveland, and Gary, Indiana, in 1967

78. Dr. Martin Luther King, Jr., received the title of doctor when he:
a. graduated from medical school
b. got his doctorate at Boston University's School of Theology

c. graduated from dental school
d. was given an honorary degree from the University of Mississippi in 1967

79. John F. Kennedy's Secretary of Defense was:
a. Robert S. McNamara
b. Clark Clifford
c. Maxwell Taylor
d. Curtis LeMay

80. Who taught primal scream therapy to John Lennon?
a. Werner Erhart
b. Eric Berne
c. Arthur Janov
d. Dr. Ruth

81. McGeorge Bundy was:
a. a Scottish cartoon that rode the crest of Beatlemania to success in America
b. the rock group—Princeton graduates—who headed the Monterey Pop Festival
c. President Johnson's National Security Advisor
d. mystery writer Ian Fleming's real name

82. Who quoted the abolitionist preacher Theodore Parker, saying, "The arc of the moral universe is long, but it bends towards justice"?
a. Robert Kennedy
b. Dr. Martin Luther King, Jr.
c. Rabbi Abraham Joshua Heschel
d. Rev. Jesse Jackson

83. Lyndon Johnson once called _____ "the Winston Churchill of South Asia."
a. Jawaharlal Nehru
b. Gandhi
c. Ngo Dinh Diem
d. Ferdinand Marcos

84. What was the name of the first policeman who tried to question Lee Harvey Oswald after Oswald shot JFK?

a. J.D. Tippit
b. M.N. McDonald
c. Lieutenant Paul Bentley
d. Captain Will Fritz

85. After the assassination of Mississippi civil rights leader Medgar Evers, the U.S. government brought charges against _____. In 1964, his trial ended in a hung jury. Who was he?
a. Sheriff Lawrence A. Rainey
b. William Calley, Jr.
c. Byron De La Beckwith
d. Chief Laurie Pritchett

86. Moses Herzog was:
a. the President of Israel during the 1967 war
b. a fictional inveterate letter writer
c. the manager of the Chicago White Sox
d. the rabbi who spoke at the 1963 March on Washington

87. "We're eyeball to eyeball, and I think the other fellow just blinked." Who said this?
a. Lyndon Johnson
b. Henry Kissinger
c. Robert F. Kennedy
d. Dean Rusk

88. In John F. Kennedy's mythology, the West Virginia primary was legendary because:
a. It was the first place Kennedy had passed out his P.T. 109 pins to followers.
b. It was the first time Kennedy had displayed his vaunted sense of humor in public.
c. It was where Kennedy discovered poverty.
d. It was the first place FDR, Jr., campaigned for him, an important link between FDR and JFK.

89. Which war protestor said, "No Vietcong ever called me nigger"?
a. Stokely Carmichael
b. H. Rap Brown
c. Malcolm X
d. Muhammad Ali

90. After clashes with the police during the 1968 Democratic Convention, protestors looked at the TV cameras and chanted:

a. "End the war in Vietnam, send the troops home."

b. "Give peace a chance."

c. "The whole world is watching."

d. "We shall overcome."

91. Timothy Leary performed his drug experiments with:

a. LSD

b. mescaline

c. cocaine

d. psilocybin

92. "Om" was a chant heard often in the streets outside the Chicago Convention. With whom was it associated?

a. Allen Ginsberg

b. Rev. Ralph D. Abernathy

c. Tom Hayden

d. Father Daniel Berrigan

93. Beginning in 1963, newspapers and magazines reported on a growing reaction against civil rights advancements. What was the media's name for that reaction?

a. the new conservatism

b. the white backlash

c. the new populism

d. the new right

94. John F. Kennedy's chief speechwriter was:

a. Richard Goodwin

b. Robert Kennedy

c. Theodore Sorensen

d. Kenneth O'Donnell

95. "Moderation in defense of freedom is no virtue. Extremism in defense of liberty is no vice." What nationally prominent politician made that proclamation?

a. Ronald Reagan, when he ran for governor of California and described his fierce opposition to the radicals.

b. Barry Goldwater, in his acceptance speech at the Republican presidential nomination in 1964.

c. Lyndon Johnson, speaking to a group of Green Berets en route to Vietnam

d. Governor George Wallace, when he announced his 1968 campaign for the presidency

96. Jacqueline Kennedy married Aristotle Onassis:
a. at Notre Dame Cathedral, Paris
b. in a private ceremony at the Vatican
c. in a private chapel on the island of Skorpios
d. at City Hall, New York City

97. In the sixties a professor of philosophy became a guru of the New Left. He believed that American tolerance was really repressive since it gave equal weight to just and unjust ideas. He was:
a. David Riesman
b. Max Lerner
c. Richard Alpert
d. Herbert Marcuse

98. Who was the doctor who was jailed for refusing to serve as a medical instructor to the Green Berets in 1967?
a. Dr. Howard Levy
b. Dr. Benjamin Spock
c. Dr. Jonas Salk
d. Dr. Janet Travell

99. Who was the first peace candidate to run for the Senate from Massachusetts?'
a. Arthur Schlesinger, Jr.
b. Father Robert Drinan
c. Professor H. Stuart Hughes
d. Warren Beatty

100. _____ was one of the leaders of the 1968 uprising of French students.
a. Red Rudi
b. Régis Debray
c. Jack Lang
d. Danny the Red

101. Abiyoyo was:

a. the African name for Tanzania's President Julius Nyerere

b. the name of the Kenyan diplomat who was refused service at a restaurant in Atlanta in 1963

c. the Swahili word for sleep

d. a song made famous by Pete Seeger

102. What politician became increasingly notorious for bottling up the Equal Rights Amendment in committee?

a. Brooklyn Congressman Emmanuel Celler

b. South Carolina Senator Strom Thurmond

c. North Carolina Senator Sam Ervin

d. Maine Senator Margaret Chase Smith

103. Who was Bashir Ahmed?

a. one of the PLO's early activists

b. the commanding general of the Egyptian forces in the Six-Day War

c. a Pakistani camel driver who visited the U.S. at the invitation of Vice President Lyndon Johnson

d. an aide to Black Muslim leader Elijah Muhammad

104. The Prague Spring was:

a. a Dvořák symphony whose lightheartedness expressed the mood of the counterculture

b. the European spa where the world's finest bottled water was produced

c. the freewheeling months before the 1968 Soviet invasion

d. Prague's grim spring of 1964

105. When he came to America in 1960, Nikita Khrushchev:

a. showed his disapproval at the United Nations by banging his shoe on a desk

b. staged a "kitchen debate" with Richard Nixon

c. went backstage after enjoying a performance of *Can Can*

d. left the Waldorf Hotel in a huff, and took a suite in Harlem's Hotel Theresa

106. In the 1960 presidential campaign, a speech in Houston, Texas, became well known. Why?

a. It was the speech in which Lyndon Johnson, angling for the

nomination, spelled out his plans for the kinds of social programs he believed were necessary. The speech laid the groundwork for the Great Society.
b. It was the speech in which Richard Nixon offered an important affirmation of the Republican Party's commitment to civil rights.
c. It was the speech in which JFK squarely confronted the issue of his Catholicism.
d. It was the speech in which President Eisenhower, campaigning hard for the Republican ticket, attacked the defense industry, calling it the "military-industrial complex."

107. General Edwin A. Walker was:
a. a onetime army general who became a member of the John Birch Society and a right-wing activist in Dallas, Texas
b. the general who subdued Nicaraguan rebels in the nineteenth century and became a symbol of U.S. imperialism for the New Left
c. a former CIA agent who was jailed for taking bribes from the Libyans
d. a former American army officer who sold military secrets to the Soviets

108. Who said he thought the U.S. would be better off if the Eastern Seaboard could be cut away and let float out to sea?
a. George Wallace
b. Ronald Reagan
c. Clint Eastwood
d. Barry Goldwater

109. When Adlai Stevenson visited Dallas in October 1963, he:
a. was greeted warmly by thousands of Democrats who had supported him in the fifties
b. was the guest at an extremely well-attended book luncheon where he discussed *To Turn the Tide,* a collection of his essays.
c. was surrounded by angry, jeering Texans before a nighttime speech and bashed on the head by a woman's placard which read, "If you seek peace, ask Jesus"
d. tried to negotiate a peace treaty between the factions of the Texas Democratic party represented by Ralph Yarborough and John Connally

110. In the early sixties Americans were urged to include _____ in their homes.
a. radiation detectors
b. fallout shelters
c. anti-aircraft weapon sites, to fight off enemy planes
d. libraries so the family could study in case a nuclear attack destroyed their schools

111. Who was kidnapped in the sixties and held in Harrah Lodge in Lake Tahoe until his father paid the ransom?
a. Frank Sinatra, Jr.
b. Gary Crosby
c. Brooke Hayward
d. Gary Lewis

112. Bobby Baker was:
a. a country music star who eclipsed Elvis in popularity in Elvis's later years
b. the football coach of Columbia University
c. a protégé of Lyndon Johnson who was tried for tax evasion and fraud
d. a protégé of Lyndon Johnson who was caught in a men's room during an alleged sexual encounter, and retired to Texas

113. In 1968 _____ retired to Bimini, where he advised friends to "Keep the faith..."
a. Bernie Cornfeld
b. Clifford Irving
c. H. Rap Brown
d. Rev. Adam Clayton Powell

114. In 1967, a woman who called herself Svetlana Allilueva arrived in America. In reality, she was:
a. the Polish film star who married journalist David Halberstam
b. the first Jewish refusenik to attain her freedom
c. a Russian spy—a latter-day Federenko
d. Svetlana Stalin

115. In 1967, in Hollybush, New Jersey:
a. thousands of black and Hispanic migrant workers began a successful strike for better pay and health conditions

b. Bruce Springsteen, still a high school student, gave his first concert

c. President Lyndon Johnson and Soviet Premier Alexei Kosygin held a summit

d. William Carlos Williams donated his papers to Glassboro State College

116. In 1967, American Nazi Party leader _____ was assassinated in a Virginia parking lot.
a. George Lincoln Rockwell
b. General Edwin A. Walker
c. Robert Welch
d. Dr. Fred Schwarz

117. Secretary of State Dean Rusk's daughter, Margaret Elizabeth Rusk, shocked many Americans when she:
a. publicly criticized the war in Vietnam
b. married a black man, Guy Gibson Smith
c. came out of the closet as a lesbian
d. auditioned for a nude scene in *Last Tango in Paris*

118. One of Dr. Christiaan Barnard's earliest heart-transplant patients was:
a. Michael DeBakey
b. Philip Blaiberg
c. Barney Clark
d. Joseph Jarvik

119. The Pueblo was:
a. the section of Denver where activists hid out after a raid in New Mexico to protest the violation of Chicano land rights
b. Helen Frankenthaler's triptych of the ruins of a New Mexican Indian pueblo
c. the first popular Chicano novel, written by Richard Sanchez
d. a naval vessel captured by the North Koreans in 1968

120. Resurrection City was:
a. the prototype for Jim Bakker's Heritage Village
b. the headquarters for the Poor People's Campaign
c. the civil rights movement's name for Jackson, Mississippi, during the 1964 Freedom Summer

d. a nickname for New York City, so called because of all the refugees who converged there

121. The night RFK was shot in Los Angeles, two star athletes were at his side. Who were they?
a. Sandy Koufax and Willie Mays
b. Willis Reed and Wilt Chamberlain
c. Billie Jean King and Arthur Ashe
d. Roosevelt Grier and Rafer Johnson

122. "Clean for Gene" was:
a. an anti-drug slogan
b. an advertising slogan for Levi's
c. the youth brigade that worked in Eugene McCarthy's presidential campaign
d. a mantra for followers of the Maharishi Mahesh Yogi

123. The Little Red Book was:
a. a book of recipes published by a leftist women's collective
b. a list of Communist Party sympathizers in the entertainment industry
c. the teachings of Chairman Mao
d. an encyclopedia of hallucinogens

124. "Ho, Ho, Ho Chi Minh, the NLF is gonna win" was:
a. a derisive chant that began at the first Superbowl
b. a chant of American student radicals
c. the headline carried by *The New York Daily News* the day Saigon fell
d. a chant made famous by Buddhist monks in Saigon

125. "Hey, Hey, LBJ, how many _____ did you kill today?"
a. VC
b. GIs
c. kids
d. peasants

126. "We had to destroy _____ to save it."
a. Hue
b. Ben Tre
c. Saigon
d. Hanoi

127. Who was among the first appointments announced by JFK in 1960:
a. Byron White
b. J. Edgar Hoover
c. Dean Rusk
d. Arthur Goldberg

128. The Pickrick Restaurant was famous for its
a. ribs
b. fried chicken
c. pickax handles
d. cheesecake

129. Who owned the Pickrick?
a. Lurleen Wallace
b. Orville Faubus
c. George Wallace
d. Lester Maddox

130. In 1965, Rolling Thunder was important. What was it?
a. an herbal tea much loved by hippies
b. the concert tour put together by Bob Dylan, featuring Joan Baez
c. the bombing operation that was supposed to bring North Vietnam to its knees
d. the heavy metal band that made its debut on *The Ed Sullivan Show* that year

131. Who coined the phrase "credibility gap"?
a. Art Buchwald
b. An editor at *The Herald Tribune*
c. Spiro Agnew
d. Normal Mailer

132. An arrest took place at the corner of Imperial Highway and Avalon Boulevard in Los Angeles. Who was arrested and why did the arrest eventually become important?
a. Charles Manson was arrested. That arrest led to the apprehension of his "family."
b. John Lennon was arrested for possession of drugs. The arrest figured prominently in the U.S. government's attempt to deport him.

c. Marquette Frye was arrested for drunk driving, touching off the Watts riot.

d. Cinque—a member of the Symbionese Liberation Army—was arrested in connection with the kidnapping of Patty Hearst.

133. The following were places that were invaded during the sixties. Match them up with their invaders:

a. Czechoslovakia	**1.** United States
b. Dominican Republic	**2.** China
c. India	**3.** Soviet Union
d. Goa	**4.** India

134. Who coined the phrase "radical chic"?
a. New York City politician Mario Procaccino
b. An editor at *The New York Times*
c. Tom Wolfe
d. Spiro Agnew

135. What was the Iron Triangle, and why was it famous?
a. It was one of the early heavy-metal bands, whose onstage theatrics and offstage nihilism were so offensive that their records were banned on most radio stations.
b. It was the area near Pittsburgh, home of U.S. Steel, which was becoming a nationwide symbol of America's declining competitiveness in manufacturing.
c. It was the three-legged consortium known collectively as Big Steel. The owners had a much-publicized meeting with JFK in which Kennedy warned them not to increase their prices.
d. It was the area north of Saigon where a major battle was fought in 1967.

136. Who called the U.S. the "greatest purveyor of violence in the world today"?
a. Mao Tse-tung
b. Dr. Martin Luther King, Jr.
c. Abbie Hoffman
d. Leonid Brezhnev

137. Who was General Lewis B. Hershey?
a. the cartoon character who advertised Hershey bars on Saturday morning TV
b. the head of the Selective Service

c. the commanding officer of U.S. forces in Vietnam
d. the commanding officer of U.S. forces in the Dominican Republic

138. Who called anti-war activists "nervous nellies"?
a. Vice President Spiro Agnew
b. President Lyndon Johnson
c. Attorney General John Mitchell
d. Presidential speechwriter Pat Buchanan

139. Who coined the phrase "benign neglect"?
a. Tom Wolfe
b. Pat Moynihan
c. an editor at *The Washington Post*
d. Attorney General John Mitchell

140. Who said, "If you give me a gun, I might just shoot Lady Bird"?
a. Abbie Hoffman
b. H. Rap Brown
c. Stokely Carmichael
d. Lester Maddox

141. What was the Revolutionary Youth Movement I?
a. the official name of the Red Guards
b. the official name of the Weathermen
c. the official name of the umbrella group that called the 1968 strikes that paralyzed Paris
d. the official name of a radical commune in Berkeley, otherwise known as the Red Family

142. Who was S.I. Hayakawa?
a. the leader of a radical Indian group in Wounded Knee, South Dakota
b. President of San Francisco State University
c. President of Columbia University
d. President of Condé-Nast Publications

143. Who referred to marriage as "legalized rape"?
a. Alan Alda
b. Ti-Grace Atkinson
c. Gloria Steinem
d. Billie Jean King

144. Who called the U.S. the Fourth Reich?
a. Ron Karenga
b. William Kunstler
c. Norman Mailer
d. James Baldwin

145. "Radical chic" told the story of a party held in New York City. At whose home was it held?
a. John Lennon's apartment at the Dakota
b. Norman Mailer's Brooklyn townhouse
c. Leonard Bernstein's Upper East Side apartment
d. William Kunstler's apartment in Greenwich Village

146. The name of the spacecraft that landed on the moon was:
a. the *Skylab*
b. the *Eagle*
c. the *Challenger*
d. the *Columbia*

147. Who said "There are a lot of mediocre judges and people... aren't they entitled to a little representation..."?
a. George Wallace
b. Spiro Agnew
c. Sen. Roman Hruska
d. Sen. Everett Dirksen

148. In what context did he say it?
a. during the Chicago conspiracy trial
b. during the confirmation hearings of Judge G. Harrold Carswell
c. during the confirmation hearings of Judge Clement F. Haynsworth
d. during the Ellsberg trial

149. Dike Bridge became famous. Why?
a. It was the scene of a lesbian rally.
b. It figured in the song by Bobbie Gentry.
c. It was the bridge Ted Kennedy drove off, killing Mary Jo Kopechne.
d. It was the bridge leading out of Washington, D.C., into the suburbs that was hit by an airliner on a snowy winter day in the middle of the evening rush hour.

150. A famous crime was committed on Cielo Drive in Los Angeles. What was the crime; who was the victim; who was the criminal?

a. Patty Hearst was kidnapped by the Symbionese Liberation Army.
b. David Begelman forged the signature on a check written to Cliff Robertson.
c. The Plumbers broke into the offices of Daniel Ellsberg's psychiatrist.
d. Sharon Tate was murdered by the Manson Family.

151. What car did Ralph Nader call "unsafe at any speed"?
a. the Ford Pinto
b. the Chevrolet Corvair
c. the Dodge Dart
d. the Volkswagen bug

152. What was the auto industry's response to Ralph Nader?
a. Volkswagen put him on their board of directors.
b. Ford ordered the car redesigned.
c. Nader charged that General Motors assigned private detectives to follow him.
d. General Motors ordered all of that year's cars recalled for testing and offered consumers a rebate.

153. One presidential son-in-law was one of Nader's Raiders. Which one was it?
a. Charles Robb
b. Patrick Nugent
c. Edward F. Cox
d. David Eisenhower

154. Which of the following did the Yippies threaten to do at the 1968 Democratic Convention in Chicago?
a. inject the city's water supply with LSD
b. send Yippie women to seduce convention delegates
c. send "hyper-potent" Yippie men to seduce the delegates' wives and daughters
d. all of the above

155. In June of 1967, how many American troops were assigned to "Support and Defense" in Vietnam?
a. 20,000
b. 50,000
c. 100,000
d. 414,000

156. In June of 1967, how many American troops were assigned to "Offensive Ground Operations" in Vietnam?
a. 50,000
b. 100,000
c. 300,000
d. 450,000

157. Nikita Khrushchev visited New York in 1960. While he was there, he appeared on one television show. Who was the host?
a. Charles Collingwood
b. Edward R. Murrow
c. David Susskind
d. Buffalo Bob

158. Who stayed at Harlem's Hotel Theresa while in New York?
a. Rev. Adam Clayton Powell
b. Fidel Castro
c. the Beatles
d. Nikita Khrushchev

159. What did CIA agents do to learn the effects of LSD on average people?
a. They interviewed physicians.
b. They tested soldiers.
c. They administered the drug to themselves.
d. In an operation called Midnight Climax, they hired San Francisco prostitutes to drug their johns.

160. Who busted Timothy Leary at Millbrook, New York?
a. John Doar
b. J. Edgar Hoover
c. Frank Serpico
d. G. Gordon Liddy

161. A number of American anti-war activists wore rings to symbolize their solidarity with the Vietnamese National Liberation Front. What were the rings made of?
a. beer can rings, popped by American GIs
b. metal from downed American airplanes
c. water buffalo whiskers
d. wood carved by Montagnard tribesmen

162. During the late sixties, even going shopping became a political event. Among the committed, grapes grown in California were forbidden, as was lettuce from the same state. Sheets and towels from the JP Stevens Co. were avoided because of the company's union-busting tactics. What other product was on the forbidden list?

a. Anything made by the Nestlé Company, because of its propaganda drive for powdered milk among new mothers in the Third World.

b. Anything made by Dow Chemical Co., because Dow Chemical produced napalm.

c. Lemons and oranges from Israel. In the wake of the Six-Day War, some radical leftists characterized Israel as an exploitive nation of Europeans victimizing the indigenous people of Palestine.

d. California wine. Made from California grapes—a logical extension of the grape boycott.

163. These are the real names. Who did they eventually turn themselves into?

a. Bob Zimmerman	**1.** Geraldo Rivera
b. Lew Alcindor	**2.** Kareem Abdul-Jabbar
c. Cassius Clay	**3.** Bob Dylan
d. Malcolm Little	**4.** Little Richard
e. Steveland Morris	**5.** Muhammad Ali
f. Richard Penniman	**6.** Stevie Wonder
g. Jerry Rivers	**7.** Malcolm X

164. What did NBC executives do when Barbara Walters told them Jackie Kennedy was about to marry Aristotle Onassis?

a. They led the evening news with the story.

b. They flew Walters to Greece for an exclusive with Onassis.

c. They refused to let her report the story because it was unbelievable.

d. They staked out Jackie's New York City apartment building.

165. Name the sixties romance that lasted:

a. Sonny and Cher

b. Elizabeth Taylor and Richard Burton

c. David Eisenhower and Julie Nixon

d. Luci Baines Johnson and Patrick Nugent

166. Beautifying America was a project dear to:
a. Pat Nixon
b. Lady Bird Johnson
c. Jacqueline Kennedy
d. Liz Carpenter

167. Which presidential son-in-law served in Vietnam?
a. Patrick Nugent
b. Charles Robb
c. David Eisenhower
d. Edward F. Cox

168. When was Andy Warhol shot?
a. the day before Robert Kennedy was shot
b. the day before Dr. Martin Luther King, Jr., was shot
c. the day before JFK was shot
d. the day before Malcolm X was shot

169. The woman who shot him, Valerie Solanis, was affiliated with S.C.U.M. What was S.C.U.M.?
a. The Society for Cutting Up Men
b. South Carolina University Museum
c. Sacred Church of Universal Meditation
d. Single Californians Upset by Mollusks

170. When asked what kind of world she hoped to create, what did Valerie Solanis say?
a. "A world safe for women."
b. "A world where men and women respect each other."
c. "An out-of-sight, groovy, all-female world."
d. She didn't say anything. Instead she burst into an improvised song: "I am woman, hear me roar."

171. Ethel Scull was:
a. a Guardian Angel
b. a Hell's Angel
c. an art collector
d. the wife of a taxi mogul in New York City

172. What was the name of the motel where Dr. Martin Luther King, Jr., was assassinated?
a. The Lurleen Motel

b. The Lorraine Motel
c. The Lucinda Motel
d. The Lincoln Motel

173. Alexander Dubček was:
a. the Polish student who was the first to be killed while trying to leap over the Berlin Wall
b. the Hungarian immigrant who protested the American Nazi Party march in Skokie, Illinois
c. a Catholic priest beaten unconscious after the march in Selma
d. the Czech leader during the Prague Spring

174. "That's one small step for man, one giant leap for _____."
a. all of us
b. the human race
c. mankind
d. earthlings

175. Who was Ramon George Sneyd?
a. That was the name on the passport James Earl Ray was carrying when he was arrested.
b. That was the name of the man who, in the early sixties, set about building the premier cocaine cartel in Colombia.
c. That was the pseudonym used by Adolf Eichmann during the time he lived in Buenos Aires.
d. That was the name Fidel Castro used as an underground revolutionary.

176. The saying "Only Hanoi knows" referred to:
a. the number of North Vietnamese regulars fighting in the South at any given time
b. the whereabouts of American MIAs
c. the number of Vietcong dead
d. the information Jane Fonda gave to her North Vietnamese hosts

177. Outside the delegates' hotels during the 1968 Democratic Convention, protesters, journalists—and delegates themselves—were beaten in what was later called a police riot. Inside his hotel, Hubert Humphrey was:
a. Furiously arguing with Chicago Mayor Richard Daley by telephone. Humphrey's point was that the indiscriminate violence

would be used against him during the campaign and might lose him the election.
b. Desperately lobbying Senator Eugene McCarthy to support him. He went so far as to offer McCarthy the job of Secretary of Defense in his administration if he would appeal to his supporters in the streets to calmly return to their hotels.
c. Watching the convention on television and savoring his moment of triumph.
d. Reporting by telephone to Lyndon Johnson. Both men agreed that Daley had shown a great deal of loyalty to the administration and deserved a reward come November.

178. Who called the Vietnam War "Christ's War"?
a. Evangelist Billy Graham
b. Richard Cardinal Cushing of Boston
c. Francis Cardinal Spellman of New York
d. Dr. Norman Vincent Peale

179. _____ sponsored the Freedom Rides.
a. NAACP
b. CORE
c. SNCC
d. SCLC

180. During a White House luncheon, _____ attacked Lady Bird Johnson because of her husband's war policies.
a. Eartha Kitt
b. Lena Horne
c. Mahalia Jackson
d. Ella Fitzgerald

181. General Giap was:
a. the vice president of the Republic of South Vietnam
b. the air force chief of staff of the Republic of South Vietnam
c. married to Madame Nhu
d. commanding officer of the North Vietnamese forces

182. "In your heart, you know he's right" was a slogan for:
a. Spiro Agnew
b. Ronald Reagan

c. George Wallace
d. Barry Goldwater

183. The Democrats answered the slogan with one of their own:
a. "In your head, you know he's wrong."
b. "In your gut, you know he's wrong."
c. "In your heart, you know he might."
d. "In your guts, you know he's nuts."

184. _____ was the first black student to enroll at Ole Miss:
a. Medgar Evers
b. James Meredith
c. Rosa Parks
d. Bob Moses

185. In the wake of the King assassination, _____ mused that the assassination of JFK had "set something loose in this country."
a. Mark Lane
b. New Orleans district attorney Jim Garrison
c. Jacqueline Kennedy
d. Robert F. Kennedy

186. Speaking of a colleague, _____ said, "He cries too much." Who said it and who was he talking about?
a. Johnny Carson said it of Jack Paar.
b. Robert Kennedy said it of Ed Muskie.
c. Lyndon Johnson said it of Hubert Humphrey.
d. Richard Nixon said it of Ed Muskie.

187. On March 16, 1968, something happened at a place nicknamed Pinkville. What happened?
a. The secret bombing campaign against Cambodia began. Pinkville was the first target.
b. Pinkville was the army's nickname for Hue after North Vietnamese troops took the city. March 16 was the day suspected enemies of the people were rounded up and executed.
c. Pinkville was the police code name for the area of Chicago where Panther leader Fred Hampton lived. March 16 was the day they broke into his apartment and shot him.
d. Pinkville was the nickname for a Vietnamese hamlet named My

Lai. March 16 was the day 567 civilians were killed there by U.S. forces.

188. Who was the officer in charge at My Lai?
a. Paul David Meadlo
b. William L. Calley, Jr.
c. Ernest Medina
d. Samuel Koster

189. Who was the commander of the *Pueblo*?
a. Creighton Abrams
b. John Paul Vann
c. Jeremiah Denton
d. Lloyd M. Bucher

Music

1. Bob Dylan was born in:
a. Greenwich Village
b. Duluth, Minnesota
c. Hibbing, Minnesota
d. The Main Line outside Philadelphia

2. Caesar and Cleo eventually became successful. Who were they?
a. Sonny and Cher
b. Delaney and Bonnie
c. The Carpenters
d. Captain and Tennille

3. Which two of these singers were the Mamas of the Mamas and the Papas?
a. Cass Elliott
b. Grace Slick
c. Mary Travers
d. Michelle Phillips

4. George Harrison's haircut in "A Hard Day's Night" was:
a. an imitation of the Maharishi's Mahesh Yogi's
b. the inspiration for Arthur, a famous nightclub in New York City
c. deliberately longer than the other Beatles'
d. a crew cut

5. "Satisfaction" was:
a. Mick Jagger's cruel ode to Marianne Faithfull
b. a self-conscious attempt to give the Rolling Stones the same world-weary sound as black blues groups
c. the Rolling Stones' first big American hit
d. the Rolling Stones' put-down of their financial advisors because they hadn't yet made a million dollars

6. Which two of the following Rolling Stones were arrested during the famous bust at the house party in the mansion, Redlands?
a. Charlie Watts
b. Keith Richards
c. Brian Jones
d. Mick Jagger

7. Match the Rolling Stones phrase to the song:
a. "Please allow me to intro-   1. "Sympathy for the Devil"
duce myself."
b. "Now I need you more than   2. "Let's Spend the Night To-
ever."   gether"
c. "Here's a song for all the hard-   3. "Salt of the Earth"
working people."
d. "I saw her today at the re-   4. "You Can't Always Get What
ception."   You Want"

8. Who was not a member of the Beatles during their first performances in Hamburg?
a. George Harrison
b. Paul McCartney
c. John Lennon
d. Ringo Starr

9. Who was the Beatles' drummer before Ringo Starr joined the Beatles?
a. Stu Sutcliffe
b. Rory Storm
c. Michael McCartney
d. Pete Best

10. What sixties rocker described himself as an "erotic politician"?
a. Mick Jagger

b. John Lennon
c. Dave Clark
d. Jim Morrison

11. If your name was Virgil Kane, what train did you work on?
a. the Denver train
b. the Danbury train
c. the Danville train
d. the Danvers train

12. Why did the Doors choose that name?
a. They took it from the title of the Aldous Huxley book about hallucinogens, *The Doors of Perception*.
b. They chose it because they liked the image of doors opening after the repression of the fifties.
c. It was a ripoff of cockney rhyming slang—the rhyme was "bores."
d. They chose it to symbolize a closed door, showing their alienation from their fans.

13. What was happening on the cover of the *Abbey Road* album?
a. The Beatles are photographed wearing black turtlenecks, with their faces shown in half-shadow.
b. The photo shows the band interspersed with various historical figures.
c. Nothing. The sleeve is plain white.
d. The band is shown crossing the street.

14. Who wrote the song "Turn! Turn! Turn!"?
a. Bob Dylan
b. Roger McGuinn
c. John Phillips
d. Pete Seeger

15. If you heard the lyrics "A white man's heaven is a black man's hell," the singer was probably:
a. Bull Connor
b. Malcolm X
c. Rev. Louis Farrakhan
d. Chubby Checker

41

16. "Raindrops Keep Falling on My Head" was:
a. the theme of *Butch Cassidy and the Sundance Kid*
b. John Denver's first hit
c. Charles Goodell's theme song during his New York Republican Senate campaign
d. a commercial for Totes umbrellas

17. In "Dear Landlord," Bob Dylan bargains with his landlord. He sings:
a. "If you don't underestimate me, I won't underestimate you."
b. "You can be in my dream if I can be in yours."
c. "Don't think twice—it's all right."
d. "I gave her my heart but she wanted my soul."

18. Joan Baez was once married to:
a. Bob Dylan
b. David Harris
c. Tom Hayden
d. no one

19. Which song was likely to "induce the American public to surrender to atheistic international Communism," according to the Christian Anti-Communist Crusade?
a. "Blowin' in the Wind"
b. "Satisfaction"
c. "Eve of Destruction"
d. "Revolution"

20. It was sung by:
a. Peter, Paul and Mary
b. Barry McGuire
c. The Beatles
d. Bob Dylan

21. In 1969 the music world was full of rumors that Paul McCartney had died. Which was *not* a piece of Beatle lore that fed these rumors?
a. The fact that Paul is shown barefoot on the cover of the *Abbey Road* album.
b. The notion that if you played "I Am a Walrus" backward, you could hear John sing "Paul is dead."

c. The fact that the *Abbey Road* album shows a parked car with the license plate reading 28 IF, which would have been Paul's age were he alive.

d. The rumor that a deranged gunman had shot Paul while on vacation in the Bahamas.

22. You hear an energetic shout and the words "Everywhere I hear the sound of _____." Fill in the missing words.

a. people in the street

b. summer in the city

c. marching, charging feet

d. dancin' in the street

23. Who sang them?

a. Martha and the Vandellas

b. The Lovin' Spoonful

c. Buffalo Springfield

d. The Rolling Stones

24. A memorial to Brian Jones was held:

a. at Westminster Abbey

b. during a free concert in Hyde Park

c. on the roof of the Apple building

d. at Stonehenge

25. "If you want someone to cream on, just cream on me" comes from:

a. *The Story of O*

b. the Rolling Stones' "You Can't Always Get What You Want"

c. the Rolling Stones' "Let It Bleed"

d. a hip commercial in which a face is talking to a jar of Pond's skin cream

26. Chip Monck was

a. Dave Garroway's pet on *The Today Show*

b. the coach of the Cleveland Browns in 1967

c. part of the Rolling Stones' entourage

d. one of the Chipmunks on the Chipmunks records

27. Who produced Mary Hopkin's 1968 hit song "Those Were the Days"?

a. Phil Spector
b. Jerry Wexler
c. John Hammond
d. Paul McCartney

28. Why did Alvin become famous?
a. It was the nickname George Harrison gave to his haircut in *A Hard Day's Night.*
b. It was the name of one of the Chipmunks on the Chipmunk records.
c. It was the name of one of the characters in *Yellow Submarine.*
d. It was the name of a trendy New York City discotheque.

29. Which of these was *not* a Beach Boys song?
a. "Surfin' Safari"
b. "California Dreamin'"
c. "California Girls"
d. "Help Me, Rhonda"

30. What was Lara's Theme?
a. the theme song from *Gone With the Wind,* which became popular again when the movie was re-released in the sixties
b. the theme song from *Dr. Zhivago*
c. the theme song for Wolfman Jack's program
d. the theme song Doc Severinson became famous for when he played it every night on *The Tonight Show*

31. By 1968 the Beach Boys lead singer, Brian Wilson, was almost as famous for his eccentricities as for his music. He:
a. had a tent erected in his living room and filled it with vegetables and tons of sand
b. rode his motorcycle so wildly that his brothers hired a bodyguard to stop his midnight rides
c. refused to eat days at a time so he could maintain his surfing shape
d. while exercising periodically signalled his wife to blow marijuana smoke through a ventilator hole in the wall

32. Before they were the Supremes, Diana Ross, Mary Wilson, Betty McGlown, Barbara Martin, and Florence Ballard were all at one time part of a group called:

a. The Primettes
b. The Tonettes
c. The Quartettes
d. The Jewelettes

33. The Supremes' first hit was:
a. "Baby Love"
b. "Where Did Our Love Go?"
c. "Stop! In the Name of Love"
d. "Back in My Arms Again"

34. Which of the following singers did *not* appear on *The Ed Sullivan Show*?
a. The Dave Clark 5
b. The Rolling Stones
c. Joan Baez
d. The Beatles

35. What happened to Florence Ballard?
a. She left the Supremes and went on to a career as a stage actress, most notably in the original production of *Ain't Misbehavin'*.
b. She left the Supremes and became a radical, finally marrying a black power leader and settling in Africa.
c. She went broke after leaving the Supremes and later died of a heart attack.
d. She left the Supremes to marry Motown president Berry Gordy.

36. Which act was *not* a Motown act?
a. The Supremes
b. Smokey Robinson and the Miracles
c. Little Stevie Wonder
d. The Ronettes

37. Who sang "The Way You Do the Things You Do"?
a. The Four Tops
b. The Temptations
c. The Miracles
d. The Isley Brothers

38. Who married Phil Spector?
a. Diana Ross, of the Supremes

b. Ronnie Bennett, of the Ronettes

c. Janet Lennon, of the Lennon Sisters

d. Mary Hopkins

39. In April 1964, the five top singles on the Billboard Top Ten chart were all Beatles songs. Which one *wasn't* among them?

a. "I Want to Hold Your Hand"

b. "She Loves You"

c. "I Saw Her Standing There"

d. "Twist and Shout"

40. The phrase "blue-eyed soul" was said to describe:

a. The Beach Boys

b. The Monkees

c. The Mamas and the Papas

d. The Rascals

41. When Motown relocated in Los Angeles, Berry Gordy produced movies. Which one of the following did he *not* produce?

a. *The Wiz*

b. *Dreamgirls*

c. *Mahogany*

d. *Lady Sings the Blues*

42. Joan Baez first made her reputation:

a. at the Newport Folk Festival

b. at Club 47 in Cambridge, Massachusetts

c. on the cover of *Time* magazine

d. when Al Capp lampooned her in his cartoons

43. She helped Bob Dylan make his reputation:

a. at Club 47

b. when she introduced him at her concerts

c. when she goaded Al Capp to bad-mouth him

d. when she introduced him to the Beatles

44. Where did Mick Jagger go to college?

a. London School of Economics

b. Oxford

c. Cambridge

d. none of the above

45. What was Hitsville?

a. the name over the door at the Motown offices in Detroit

b. the nickname given to Graceland by Colonel Parker

c. the new name of Liverpool's Cavern Club, which was rechristened after the Beatles became famous

d. the nickname boosters gave Detroit after the Motown sound took off

46. Dweezil was:

a. a lyric in *The Fantasticks*

b. Frank Zappa's son

c. a nickname for astronaut Alan Shepard

d. the first home run hit in the Astrodome

47. When Grace Slick recorded "White Rabbit," she:

a. sounded a heartfelt tribute to her favorite childhood book, *Alice in Wonderland*

b. sought to convince the Disney studio to let her sing the part of an animal in its next cartoon

c. signalled the pleasure she got from drugs

d. transformed her carefully coded love song to the Doors' Jim Morrison into an anthem in support of the rock revolution

48. Which of these people did *not* influence the Beatles in the sixties?

a. Chuck Berry

b. the Maharishi Mahesh Yogi

c. Jesus Christ

d. Brian Epstein

49. Match the singer with the locale:

a. Simon and Garfunkel   **1.** Detroit

b. Elvis Presley   **2.** Forest Hills, New York

c. Aretha Franklin   **3.** Los Angeles

d. The Beach Boys   **4.** Memphis

50. If you were at Woodstock, you knew Wavy Gravy as:

a. the welcome call that lunch was ready

b. a new hairdo, a fad that swept the encampment

c. a rock group whose sound was even more appealingly American than the Grateful Dead's

d. a poet and social activist who headed the group called the Hog Farm

51. One of the most remarkable moments at Woodstock was a rendition of "Here Comes the Sun." Who sang it?
a. Jimi Hendrix
b. Richie Havens
c. Wavy Gravy
d. Abbie Hoffman

52. Janis Joplin's drink of choice was:
a. Tanqueray gin
b. Southern Comfort
c. B and B brandy
d. Smirnoff vodka

53. What singer, who worked closely with Dr. Martin Luther King, Jr., sang "Precious Love" at his funeral?
a. Pete Seeger
b. Mahalia Jackson
c. Aretha Franklin
d. Peter Yarrow

54. If you were a regular at the Peppermint Lounge, you waited for Joey Dee and the Starlighters so you could dance:
a. the Frug
b. the Mashed Potato
c. the Twist
d. the Locomotion

55. Which of these groups got its start in John Mayall's Blues-breakers?
a. Led Zeppelin
b. The Animals
c. Fleetwood Mac
d. The Butterfield Blues Band

56. Jim Morrison is buried in:
a. London
b. New York
c. Los Angeles
d. Paris

57. Jimi Hendrix died on September 18, 1970, in:
a. London
b. New York
c. Los Angeles
d. Paris

58. The Wall of Sound was:
a. the 1968 Chicago Bears line
b. Phil Spector's name for his music
c. the sound that came out of San Francisco in the late sixties
d. George Martin's way of layering track over track to create the Beatles' sound

59. Whose solo debut was greeted with headlines that called him "Mau, Mau, Wild Man of Borneo"?
a. Jimi Hendrix
b. Muhammad Ali
c. Donnie Osmond
d. Hugh Masekela

60. Match the performer with the birthplace:
a. Seattle, Washington   1. Stevie Wonder
b. Macon, Georgia   2. Jimi Hendrix
c. Rolling Fork, Mississippi   3. Muddy Waters
d. Saginaw, Michigan   4. Little Richard

61. Paul Simon and Art Garfunkel recorded their first single under the name of:
a. Simon and Garfunkel
b. Tom and Jerry
c. Buddy Holly
d. Paul and Artie

62. Which of the Rolling Stones first brought the group together?
a. Brian Jones
b. Mick Jagger
c. Charlie Watts
d. Keith Richards

63. In London in the sixties signs were posted on lampposts and walls saying "_____ is God." Who was it?
a. Eric Clapton

b. John Lennon
c. David Bailey
d. Harold Wilson

64. How many babies were born at Woodstock?
a. five
b. three
c. twenty
d. one

65. How many people came to Woodstock?
a. 15,000
b. 100,000
c. 400,000
d. 1,000,000

66. How many people died at Woodstock?
a. twelve
b. twenty
c. three
d. one

67. "When you're rockin' and rollin' you don't hear your mama callin' "—what was the real name of the man who sang that?
a. George Fenniman
b. Richard Penniman
c. Abbie Hoffman
d. Richard Alpert

68. Janis Joplin died of a drug overdose on October 4, 1970, in:
a. London
b. Paris
c. New York
d. Los Angeles

69. Brian Jones died in his swimming pool on July 3, 1969, in:
a. London
b. Hampshire
c. Los Angeles
d. Paris

70. Phil Ochs hanged himself on April 9, 1976, in:

a. Chicago
b. Los Angeles
c. Far Rockaway, New York
d. Detroit

71. Quality Control was:
a. a rock group that spun off from John Mayall's Bluesbreakers
b. the technique George Martin used in recording sessions with the Beatles
c. the method Andrew Oldham used in choosing groupies for the Rolling Stones
d. the division of Motown that selected records that were likely to be hits

72. Smokey Robinson and the Miracles' first big hit was:
a. "You've Really Got a Hold on Me"
b. "Shop Around"
c. "The Love I Saw in You Was Just a Mirage"
d. "Ooo Baby Baby"

73. Which of these songs was *not* a hit in early 1967?
a. "Bridge Over Troubled Water"—Simon and Garfunkel
b. "Respect"—Aretha Franklin
c. "Good Vibrations"—The Beach Boys
d. "Strawberry Fields"—The Beatles

74. Who Wrote "Respect"?
a. Otis Redding
b. Aretha Franklin
c. Marvin Gaye
d. Berry Gordy

75. Father McKenzie was:
a. the rector in *The Thorn Birds*; the theme song from the TV mini-series later became a hit
b. one of the first priests of the Catholic left to pour his blood on draft cards; Bob Dylan wrote a song about him, which he sang at the Newport Folk Festival, touching off a riot
c. the clergyman who presided over Eleanor Rigby's funeral
d. a black minister in Detroit who led a locally popular gospel group that later recorded with Motown

76. Who released "Louie, Louie" in 1961?
a. The Four Tops
b. The Kingsmen
c. Bill Haley and the Comets
d. The Rascals

77. "Ferry Cross the Mersey" was recorded by:
a. The Beatles
b. Gerry and the Pacemakers
c. The Dave Clark Five
d. Herman's Hermits

78. What album heralded Bob Dylan's post-motorcycle-crash declaration of his health?
a. *Bringing It All Back Home*
b. *Blonde on Blonde*
c. *John Wesley Harding*
d. *Street-Legal*

79. On one of his albums, Van Morrison offered special thanks to:
a. Timothy Leary
b. Sri Chinmoy
c. Chugyang Rimpoche
d. L. Ron Hubbard

80. "Who'll stop the rain?" was:
a. the introduction to a comic TV ad about the weather
b. a Bob Dylan song
c. a civil rights anthem
d. a Creedence Clearwater Revival hit

81. In 1964 Sam Cooke was at the height of his career. He had established his own management company, his own record company, and had just recorded "A Change Is Gonna Come." Then he died suddenly on December 11. What cut his life short?
a. He was shot in a motel in Los Angeles.
b. He died of a drug overdose in Chicago.
c. His plane crashed on the way to a concert in Cleveland.
d. He was assassinated by a white gang after a concert in Macon, Georgia.

82. _____ and _____ wrote the lyrics for "Will You Love Me Tomorrow?" and "Up on the Roof."
a. Adolph Green and Betty Comden
b. Burt Bacharach and Hal David
c. Carole King and Gerry Goffin
d. Jerry Leiber and Mike Stoller

83. _____ recorded "If I Were a Carpenter"?
a. Richie Havens
b. Van Morrison
c. The Byrds
d. Jimi Hendrix

84. Which record company executive brought Aretha Franklin from a Detroit church into stardom?
a. Motown's Berry Gordy
b. Columbia's John Hammond
c. Atlantic's Ahmet Ertegun
d. Arista's Clive Davis

85. Kinky Friedman founded a band called:
a. Kinky Friedman and the Texas Jewboys
b. The Kinks
c. The Grasshoppers
d. The New Monkees

86. A hootenanny was:
a. a hideaway in Scotland
b. a time when good ol' boys could kick back their heels and party
c. a technique for calling owls at night
d. a folk music jamboree

87. Who "rode forever 'neath the streets of Boston"?
a. Paul Revere's ghost in Massachusetts legend
b. Charlie on the MTA
c. Ichabod Crane
d. This was the slogan New York City transit workers used during the 1965 strike.

88. Who sang "Dominique"?
a. Edith Piaf

b. Bobby Vee
c. The Singing Nun
d. Eartha Kitt

89. Holland-Dozier-Holland was:
a. the advertising agency that developed the Marlboro Man
b. one of Motown's preeminent songwriting teams
c. the team of computer engineers who developed the synthesizer
d. the management team who ran the business side of Apple just after Brian Epstein died

90. Which Elvis Presley hit has a long, spoken narrative in the middle of the song?
a. "It's Now or Never"
b. "Heartbreak Hotel"
c. "Are You Lonesome Tonight?"
d. "Don't Be Cruel"

91. What was Elvis Presley doing professionally between 1961 and 1968, years when he didn't have a hit song, or appear in a live performance?
a. nothing—honing his skills as a gourmet cook
b. nothing—living off his royalties in Graceland
c. making movies
d. speaking out against alcohol abuse

92. "I Got You Babe" was sung by:
a. Bob Dylan
b. Sonny and Cher
c. The Supremes
d. The Rascals

93. The Byrd's song "Turn! Turn! Turn!" was:
a. an appeal to people who were against the war in Vietnam to change their ways
b. based on a spinning nineteenth-century waltz
c. based on the Book of Ecclesiastes
d. about a colorful kite spinning in the heavens.

94. In the song "Ode to Billy Joe," what bridge did Billy Joe McAllister jump off?

a. the Tallahatchie
b. the Edmund Pettus
c. the Verrazano
d. the Golden Gate

95. Who wrote Peter, Paul and Mary's hit song "For Lovin' Me"?
a. Gordon Lightfoot
b. Tom T. Hall
c. Arlo Guthrie
d. John Denver

96. Eleanor Rigby was:
a. the second president of NOW
b. the woman in the song "She's Leaving Home"
c. part of Sgt. Pepper's Lonely Hearts Club
d. a song on the *Revolver* album

97. Which song was not a Glen Campbell hit?
a. "Gentle on My Mind"
b. "By the Time I Get to Phoenix"
c. "Early Morning Rain"
d. "Wichita Lineman"

98. Max Yasgur was:
a. a pig farmer in Woodstock, New York
b. a cattle rancher in Santa Barbara, California
c. the main character in the Dylan song "Maggie's Farm"
d. a dairy farmer in Bethel, New York

99. Who did not appear at the Monterey Pop Festival?
a. The Rolling Stones
b. Janis Joplin
c. The Who
d. Jimi Hendrix

100. As opposition to the war heated up, patriotism—or the lack of it—became a major issue. Against that backdrop, there was a celebrated performance of "The Star-Spangled Banner." Who performed it and where?
a. the New Christy Minstrels, at the White House

b. the Yippies, in Chicago, during the Democratic Convention
c. the Young Americans for Freedom, at the Republican Convention
d. Jimi Hendrix, at Woodstock

101. Who was Stu Sutcliffe, and what happened to him?
a. He was an original member of the Rolling Stones; he drowned in a swimming pool after a drug overdose.
b. He was one of the original Beatles; he died of a brain tumor.
c. He was one of the promoters at Woodstock; in the aftermath of the festival, he declared bankruptcy.
d. He was the record promoter who discovered Bob Dylan; he made a fortune.

102. Who wondered if he was "moral enough to join the army, burn women, kids, houses, villages..."
a. Bob Dylan
b. Peter Yarrow
c. John Phillips
d. Arlo Guthrie

103. Who said, "I'm for anything that gets you through the night—booze or religion."
a. John Lennon
b. Father Philip Berrigan
c. Frank Sinatra
d. Paul Newman

104. Who said, "The blues is a chair..."
a. Otis Redding
b. John Hammond
c. Aretha Franklin
d. John Lennon

105. At Monterey Pop, Jimi Hendrix became famous in the U.S. for a performance where he:
a. took off his clothes and performed naked
b. threatened to leave the stage if the audience didn't calm down. Later, a spectator was stabbed to death.
c. burned his guitar
d. smashed his guitar over the head of the drummer

106. On the album cover of *Abbey Road* the four Beatles are in line; if they hold the formation, who will get to the other side first?
a. Ringo
b. John
c. George
d. Paul

107. What was Big Pink?
a. the band that backed up Bob Dylan in his early concerts
b. the house in West Saugerties, New York, where The Band recorded their first album
c. the recording studio where Bob Dylan recorded his first three albums
d. the street name for an early form of LSD

108. What was the relationship between Richard Fariña, who wrote "Been Down So Long It Looks Like Up to Me," and Joan Baez?
a. They were lovers.
b. They were childhood friends.
c. They performed together at the Newport Folk Festival.
d. They were in-laws. Fariña was married to Baez's sister, Mimi.

109. John Lennon appeared in a 1967 movie without the other Beatles. What was the name of the movie?
a. *Performance*
b. *What Did You Do in the War, Daddy?*
c. *How I Won the War*
d. *Darling*

110. What was Mae West's question when she was asked to be on the album cover of *Sgt. Pepper's Lonely Hearts Club Band*?
a. Who are the Beatles?
b. Who is Dr Pepper?
c. What would I be doing in a lonely hearts club?
d. Why do I have to wear a uniform?

111. What famous figure did the head of EMI Records remove from the *Sgt. Pepper* album cover for fear of offending large numbers of customers?
a. Adolf Hitler

b. Benedict Arnold
c. Idi Amin
d. Gandhi

112. Which college did Lesley Gore attend?
a. UCLA
b. Santa Monica City
c. Sarah Lawrence
d. University of Tennessee

113. When he wasn't writing funny songs, Tom Lehrer was:
a. an investment banker
b. a mathematician at Harvard
c. an insurance salesman in Hartford
d. a dress designer

114. The Brill Building was famous. Why?
a. It was the corporate headquarters of the hair tonic company that produced Brylcream, whose jingle was a familiar part of radio shows during the early sixties.
b. It was the site of a famous anti-war demonstration, where New York City construction workers attacked demonstrators with baseball bats. The demonstration was later commemorated in a popular song.
c. It was the home of several rock 'n' roll music publishers.
d. It was the New York City apartment house where many rock stars eventually bought apartments.

115. Which pair does *not* belong in this list?
a. Goffin and King
b. Leiber and Stroller
c. Lennon and McCartney
d. Nichols and May

116. Who wrote "Who Put the Bomp?"
a. Barry Mann
b. Carole King
c. Jerry Leiber
d. Johnny Cash

117. The Rascals sang which of the following songs?

a. "Good Lovin'"
b. "I Ain't Gonna Eat Out My Heart Anymore"
c. "Mustang Sally"
d. all of the above

118. The Godfather of Soul was:
a. Little Richard
b. Elvis Presley
c. Jerry Lee Lewis
d. James Brown

119. Sweetheart of the Rodeo was:
a. a song by The Band
b. an album by the Byrds
c. a song sung by Loretta Lynn
d. a song written by Johnny Cash

120. Eric Burdon sang with
a. The Animals
b. Eric Clapton
c. The Kinks
d. The Byrds

121. "People Get Ready" was written by:
a. Lester Chambers
b. Burt Bacharach
c. Wilson Pickett
d. Curtis Mayfield

122. Who did the drawing that appears on the album cover of *Music from Big Pink*?
a. Levon Helm's son
b. Robbie Robertson's daughter
c. The Band, collaborating on acid
d. Bob Dylan

123. In the song "Alice's Restaurant," Arlo Guthrie was arrested for:
a. burning his draft card
b. littering
c. sitting in at an ROTC building at Harvard
d. refusing to be sworn into the army

124. John and Yoko staged two bed-ins for peace. Where were they held?
a. Toronto and Amsterdam
b. London and Tokyo
c. Amsterdam and Montreal
d. New York and Montreal

125. Who wrote the song "Woodstock"?
a. Joni Mitchell
b. Crosby, Stills, Nash and Young
c. Leonard Cohen
d. James Taylor

126. Who wrote the Frank Sinatra hit "My Way"?
a. Burt Bacharach
b. Nancy Sinatra
c. Paul Anka
d. Stephen Sondheim

127. Who was head of A&R for Apple Records in 1968:
a. Brian Epstein
b. Andrew Oldham
c. Allen Klein
d. Peter Asher

128. Who wrote "Raindrops Keep Fallin' on My Head"?
a. Randy Newman
b. Carole King
c. Burt Bacharach
d. Paul Anka

129. Who was the founder of the Institute for the Study of Non-violence?
a. Dr. Martin Luther King, Jr.
b. Joan Baez
c. John Lennon
c. Pete Seeger

130. Brian Wilson ran a store in the late sixties. What was its name; what did it sell; where was it?
a. It was a clothing store, called Salad Dressing, in Malibu.

b. It was a health-food store, called the Radiant Radish, in West Hollywood.

c. It was a kite store, called Colors of the Wind, in Santa Monica.

d. It was a record store, called Disc-O-Mat, in Hawthorne, California.

131. Where was the Beatles' last live performance?

a. on the roof of the Apple building in London

b. by the side of a highway, during the Magical Mystery Tour

c. outside the EMI studio on Abbey Road

d. on a beach in the Bahamas, during the filming of *Help!*

132. Who was famous for doing the "duckwalk"?

a. Michael Jackson

b. Chuck Berry

c. Chubby Checker

d. The Ronettes

133. Marvin Gaye recorded "Ain't No Mountain High Enough" with:

a. Diana Ross

b. Mary Wells

c. Mary Wilson

d. Tammi Terrell

134. Who was not signed by Apple Records in the late sixties?

a. James Taylor

b. Carly Simon

c. Mary Hopkin

c. Badfinger

135. Pressure was put on Mick Jagger to change the lyrics of one of the Stones' songs for an appearance on *The Ed Sullivan Show.* When asked what words he'd actually sung, Jagger said, "I sang mumble." Which song was it?

a. "Satisfaction"

b. "Mother's Little Helper"

c. "Let's Spend the Night Together"

d. "Brown Sugar"

136. What was the biggest-selling Beatles' single?

a. "I Want to Hold Your Hand"

b. "Hey Jude"
c. "Strawberry Fields"
d. "Twist and Shout"

137. "Society's Child" was a song about:
a. child abuse
b. an interracial love affair
c. welfare mothers
d. a debutante

138. Who claimed that Robert Kennedy's funeral inspired him to stop working and sell his possessions?
a. Dion DiMucci
b. Bobby Darin
c. Brian Wilson
d. Jim Morrison

139. Delaney and Bonnie's Friends did *not* include:
a. Eric Clapton
b. Paul McCartney
c. Leon Russell
d. George Harrison

140. Who referred to his attempt to run a clothing store as "western communism"?
a. Brian Wilson
b. Brian Epstein
c. Brian Jones
d. Paul McCartney

141. Lady Soul was:
a. Diana Ross
b. Tina Turner
c. Aretha Franklin
d. Florence Ballard

142. Brother Love's Traveling Salvation Show was:
a. an attempt by The Band to imitate the success of *Sgt. Pepper*
b. a rock opera by Creedence Clearwater Revival
c. a Broadway show that attempted to cash in on the popularity of *Hair*
d. a song by Neil Diamond

143. Which group was known for the chant that began, "Gimme an F..."?
a. The Doors
b. The Fugs
c. Country Joe and the Fish
d. The Rolling Stones

144. Which was *not* a Blood, Sweat and Tears hit?
a. "Proud Mary"
b. "You've Made Me So Very Happy"
c. "And When I Die"
d. "Spinning Wheel"

145. Match the children with their parents:
a. Sonny and Cher
b. Tiny Tim and Miss Vicki
c. Frank and Gail Zappa
d. Grace Slick and Paul Kantner
e. Ringo Starr and Maureen Cox
f. Mick Jagger and Bianca Perez Morena de Macias
g. Country Joe McDonald and Robin Menken

1. China
2. Zak
3. Chastity
4. Seven
5. Jade
6. Tulip
7. Moon Unit

146. What was the title of the song that first brought the Beatles to Brian Epstein's attention?
a. "Twist and Shout"
b. "Roll Over Beethoven"
c. "My Bonnie"
d. "I Saw Her Standing There"

147. James Taylor had three siblings who became musicians. Who was *not* one of them?
a. Kate
b. Linc
c. Livingston
d. Alex

148. What happened at 34th and Vine?
a. Michelle Phillips met Cass Elliott.
b. That was the address of the L.A. rock club On the Rox.

c. Love Potion #9 was sold.

d. That was the corner that was home to Schwab's Drugstore, where Lana Turner was discovered.

149. Cilla Black started out as:

a. Brian Epstein's secretary

b. a drama student, a friend of Jane Asher's

c. a fashion model, a protégée of Twiggy's

d. a hatcheck girl at the Cavern Club

150. Who wrote the song "Suzanne"?

a. Rod McKuen

b. Leonard Cohen

c. Kahlil Gibran

d. Donovan

151. The Ad Lib was a famous rock club. Where was it?

a. New York

b. London

c. Liverpool

d. Los Angeles

152. Who sang "The Ballad of the Green Berets"?

a. Johnny Cash

b. Barry Sadler

c. Robin Moore

d. John Wayne

153. The Linda Ronstadt hit "Different Drum" was written by:

a. Paul McCartney of the Beatles

b. Roger McGuinn of the Byrds

c. John Phillips of the Mamas and the Papas

d. Mike Nesmith of the Monkees

Theater and Cabaret

1. In the early sixties, long-playing comedy records were in vogue. Who recorded *The Button-Down Mind of* _____ _____?
a. Vaughn Meader
b. Steve Allen
c. Bob Newhart
d. Flip Wilson

2. In what show was "What Kind of Fool Am I?" sung?
a. *The Fantasticks*
b. *Stop the World—I Want to Get Off*
c. *Hair*
d. *A Funny Thing Happened on the Way to the Forum*

3. "Send in the Clowns" was:
a. the theme song for the 1967 Ringling Brothers, Barnum and Bailey Circus
b. the theme song of Wolfman Jack's late-night radio show
c. written for the Broadway production of *A Little Night Music*
d. a pre-World War II French torch song

4. Whose imitations of John F. Kennedy became a national fad?
a. Vaughn Monroe
b. Ralph Vaughan Williams
c. Sarah Vaughan
d. Vaughn Meader

5. If you heard someone say, "I can't leave home without a passport," you were probably:
a. being arrested by the FBI en route to Cuba
b. suspected of harboring Black Panthers in your home
c. in the audience of the Living Theater
d. at a performance of *Marat/Sade*

6. Which is not a lyric from *Hair*?
a. "The age of Aquarius"
b. "What a piece of work is man"
c. "Let the sunshine in"
d. "Up, up, and away"

7. *The Trial of the Catonsville Nine* was:
a. a TV miniseries in which nine Maryland housewives formed a consciousness-raising group to liberate themselves from the drudgery of their lives
b. a play about the trial of nine members of the Catholic left who were charged with pouring blood on draft files in Catonsville, Maryland
c. an off-Broadway hit about the trial of nine Confederate prison guards
d. a sardonic movie about the arrest of nine friends who were arrested on their way to an anti-war demonstration in Washington

8. Firesign Theatre was:
a. the Los Angeles Repertory Company where *Marat/Sade* and *Equus* made their debuts
b. a Native American group that was determined to make tribal ways the centerpiece of their plots
c. a comedy group whose records had a cult following
d. the slapstick send-ups of Western movies that influenced Mel Brooks when he made *Blazing Saddles*

9. Barbra Streisand first appeared on Broadway in:
a. *Funny Girl*
b. *Flora the Red Menace*
c. *Cactus Flower*
d. *I Can Get It for You Wholesale*

10. She played:
a. Fanny Brice

b. Miss Marmelstein
c. Flora
d. none of the above

11. Whose work was part of *Oh! Calcutta!*
a. John Lennon
b. Leonard Bernstein
c. Bob Dylan
d. Kenneth Tynan

12. Julian Beck and Judith Malina were the forces behind:
a. The Group Theater
b. Café Theater
c. The Living Theater
d. The Open Theater

13. *The Royal Hunt of the Sun* featured:
a. Richard Burton
b. Christopher Plummer
c. Robert Goulet
d. Richard Chamberlain

14. The star of *Camelot* was:
a. Tom Jones
b. Richard Burton
c. Andy Williams
d. Sir John Gielgud

15. "People" was a hit song from:
a. *Hair*
b. *Funny Girl*
c. *Cabaret*
d. *The Fantasticks*

16. Who was not part of the FTA Revue?
a. Jane Fonda
b. Donald Sutherland
c. Country Joe McDonald
d. Peter Fonda

17. One European songwriter had a long-running musical named after him/her. Who was it?

a. Bertolt Brecht
b. Jacques Brel
c. Sylvie Vartan
d. Kurt Weill

18. When Irish playwright Brendan Behan died in 1964, he was working on:
a. *The Hostage*
b. a theatrical adaptation of *Borstal Boy*
c. *Richard's Cork Leg*
d. *The Quare Fellow*

19. Neil Simon's first play was:
a. *Barefoot in the Park*
b. *Come Blow Your Horn*
c. *Plaza Suite*
d. *California Suite*

20. Liza Minnelli first appeared on Broadway in:
a. *I Am a Camera*
b. *Cactus Flower*
c. *Flora the Red Menace*
d. *Cabaret*

21. *The Deputy* was:
a. a controversial play about Pope Pius XII's actions during the Holocaust
b. the play on which *The Magnificent Seven* was based
c. a controversial play about Adolf Eichmann
d. a controversial play about treatment of Native Americans at Wounded Knee

22. David Merrick and Gower Champion produced:
a. *Hair*
b. the rock opera *Tommy*
c. *Bye Bye Birdie*
d. *Oh! Calcutta!*

23. *After the Fall* was:
a. Neil Simon's autobiographical play
b. Arthur Miller's autobiographical play

c. Joe Orton's autobiographical play

d. Lillian Hellman's autobiographical play

24. Which one was *not* a Joe Orton play?

a. *Entertaining Mr. Sloane*

b. *Loot*

c. *Look Back in Anger*

d. *What the Butler Saw*

25. Joseph Papp is the founder of New York's:

a. Circle Repertory Company

b. Shakespeare Festival

c. Cafe La Mama

d. Lincoln Center Repertory Company

26. Jose Quintero became well known for his productions of:

a. Arthur Miller's plays

b. Lillian Hellman's plays

c. Sam Shepard's plays

d. Eugene O'Neill's plays

27. The Ridiculous Theatrical Company was:

a. a mime troupe based in San Francisco

b. a Boston-based puppet theater

c. a New York City avant-garde theater troupe

d. the repertory company based at Washington, D.C.'s, Kennedy Center

28. In the sixties, Jason Robards, Jr., did *not* appear in:

a. *Toys in the Attic*

b. *A Thousand Clowns*

c. *The Iceman Cometh*

d. *After the Fall*

29. Tom Stoppard's first successful play was:

a. *The Real Inspector Hound*

b. *Rosencrantz and Guildenstern Are Dead*

c. *Travesties*

d. *The Real Thing*

Literature and Journalism

1. James Kunen's *The Strawberry Statement* was:
a. a fanciful book about the relationship between summer camps and the New Left
b. a summertime dessert cookbook, particularly popular because a man had written it
c. a fanciful book about the 1968 student uprising at Columbia
d. a Yippie manifesto

2. Who wrote *Up the Down Staircase*?
a. Dr. Benjamin Spock
b. Bel Kaufman
c. Michael Jackson
d. Anne Roiphe

3. *Rush to Judgment* was the first popular book to assert that there had been a conspiracy to kill JFK. Who wrote it?
a. New Orleans District Attorney Jim Garrison
b. comedian Mort Sahl
c. right-wing journalist Ralph de Toledano
d. lawyer/activist Mark Lane

4. Who popularized the phrase "polymorphous perversion"?
a. Henry Miller in *Tropic of Capricorn*
b. Norman O. Brown in *Life Against Death*
c. Norman Mailer in *Advertisements for Myself*
d. Terry Southern in *Candy*

5. In *Portnoy's Complaint* Alexander Portnoy masturbated in:
a. a piece of liver
b. the wrapper of a Mounds bar
c. his sister's bra
d. all of the above

6. What was the catch in *Catch-22*?
a. That you couldn't get out of the army by claiming insanity. If you were sane enough to try to get out, then you weren't really insane.
b. That you couldn't ever go AWOL; one of the catchers would catch you.
c. It was in the rye.
d. There wasn't one.

7. *The French Lieutenant's Woman* was a hardcover bestseller. Its list price was:
a. $7.95
b. $10.00
c. $14.90
d. $18.00

8. What was *Ramparts'* top investigative scoop of the sixties?
a. the Pentagon Papers
b. news that the CIA had infiltrated the National Students' Association
c. news that the CIA was trying to infiltrate the rock 'n' roll industry
d. Owsley's LSD formula

9. When John H. Griffin wrote *Black Like Me*, he:
a. perfected his Southern accent so that Southerners wouldn't perceive him as a Northern liberal
b. served as an apprentice to Louis Lomax and James Baldwin to describe prejudice in America
c. dyed his skin to "pass" as black
d. produced one of the first documentaries to be shot from a black man's point of view

10. In *The Autobiography of Malcolm X*, Malcolm modelled his title and based many of his symbols on the autobiography of which American?
a. Tom Paine
b. Benjamin Franklin

c. Frederick Douglass
d. Marcus Garvey

11. Who wrote *Why Are We in Vietnam?*
a. Tom Hayden
b. Hubert Humphrey
c. Norman Mailer
d. Arthur Schlesinger, Jr.

12. Superman Comes to the Supermarket was:
a. an article about John F. Kennedy by Norman Mailer
b. a book about Mickey Mantle by Robert Daley
c. an article about a stock car race by Tom Wolfe
d. an analysis of cowboy movies by Pauline Kael

13. Match the character with the novel:
a. Oedipa Maas   1. *To Kill a Mockingbird*
b. Yossarian   2. *On the Road*
c. Holden Caulfield   3. *The Crying of Lot 49*
d. Boo Radley   4. *Catcher in the Rye*
e. Dean Moriarty   5. *Catch-22*

14. Which of the following is not associated with Norman Podhoretz?
a. *Commentary* magazine
b. *My Negro Problem and Ours*
c. *Making It*
d. *Advertisements for Myself*

15. Germaine Greer was the author of:
a. *Sexual Politics*
b. *The Female Eunuch*
c. *The Feminine Mystique*
d. *Against Our Will*

16. At the height of the war, which aboveground publication put a famous drawing of a Molotov cocktail—complete with recipe—on its cover?
a. *Esquire*
b. *The New Yorker*
c. *New York* magazine
d. *The New York Review of Books*

17. Jack Newfield's *The Prophetic Minority* was:
a. an indictment of New York City's real estate developers
b. a book about the visionary liberal wing of the Democratic party
c. a book about the early days of the New Left
d. an ironic title for his first "Ten Worst Judges" list

18. If you were in a heated discussion of an essay called "Notes on Camp" in the mid-sixties, you were talking about:
a. Susan Sontag's attempt to describe a new sensibility, which valued the artificial and exaggerated
b. Hannah Arendt's assertion that Adolf Eichmann's treatment of Eastern European Jews represented the banality of evil
c. the new fad for health food, backpacking, and outdoor living
d. the article that discussed the phenomenal success of Allen Sherman's hit that went, "Hello Mudda, hello Fadda, here I am at Camp Granada?"

19. *Armies of the Night* is a book about:
a. the war in the Mekong Delta
b. a demonstration at the Pentagon
c. young prostitutes in New York City
d. North Vietnamese guerrillas

20. When James Baldwin wrote *The Fire Next Time* he was reporting on:
a. his childhood as a boy preacher in Harlem
b. the weeks he spent with Dr. Martin Luther King, Jr., in Alabama
c. his encounters with Black Muslim leader Elijah Muhammad
d. his meetings with Richard Wright in Paris

21. Studs Terkel is:
a. a character invented by the novelist James Farrell
b. a Chicago interviewer and writer
c. a Massachusetts Congressman whose homosexuality was inadvertently disclosed
d. the hero of *The Cincinnati Kid*

22. Before Tom Wolfe became a journalist, he was:
a. a fashion stylist in San Francisco
b. a student in Yale's American Studies program
c. a stock car driver in North Carolina
d. a doorman in Chicago's fashionable Near North Side

23. In his essay "The White Negro," Norman Mailer proposed the idea that:

a. All Negroes wanted to be white.

b. America would be better off as a miscegenated country.

c. The difference between fair-skinned and dark-skinned blacks was more important than the difference between blacks and whites.

d. Repressed white America needed a dose of the Negro's free spirit to liberate itself.

24. Which of the following authors did not run for citywide office in New York?

a. Norman Mailer

b. William F. Buckley

c. George Plimpton

d. Jimmy Breslin

25. Listen to the Warm was:

a. John Lennon's first book

b. Lufthansa's slogan for its Caribbean flights

c. the slogan of the Esalen brochure

d. a Rod McKuen book

26. The Greening of America was:

a. an article that ran in *House & Garden* and sparked a gardening fad

b. a Rockefeller Foundation—supported effort to help rural areas in Maine, Appalachia, and the Mississippi Delta produce and distribute more food—it got a great deal of coverage as an alternative to the government-sponsored War on Poverty programs

c. a book about America's new youthful openness by Charles Reich

d. a coloring book designed by Charles Schultz, the creator of Snoopy

27. Kahlil Gibran was:

a. a Lebanese-born tennis player who won the French Open in 1965 and 1966; his autobiography was a bestseller in the sixties

b. a brand of hashish that Vietnam veterans smuggled into the U.S. from Laos; it became well known after *The Los Angeles Times* ran a series on it

c. the author of *The Prophet*

d. the town in Ghana where Kwame Nkrumah and Sekou Touré first met to discuss socialism in Africa

28. Jean-Paul Sartre's autobiography, published just before he won and rejected the Nobel Prize, was called:
a. *The Words*
b. *Nausea*
c. *Age of Reason*
d. *No Exit*

29. If you were at college in the early sixties and were turned on by Kierkegaard and Camus, you were:
a. a millenarian
b. an existentialist
c. a logical positivist
d. a dialectical materialist

30. In Terry Southern's *Candy,* Candy's last name was:
a. Stripe
b. Puss
c. Dancer
d. Christian

31. Soon after she leaves home and moves to Greenwich Village, Candy has an intense coupling with:
a. a hunchback
b. a dwarf
c. an albino
d. a doctor who teaches masturbation

32. In J.D. Salinger's *Franny and Zooey,* what prayer did Franny Glass recite repeatedly when she came home from college and had a breakdown?
a. the Buddhist prayer "Om shanti"
b. the Jesus Prayer
c. the Hindu chant "Hare Krishna"
d. the Hopi Indian prayer for inner peace

33. Zooey chastizes Franny after she:
a. refuses to eat their mother's "consecrated chicken soup"
b. decides to make a pilgrimage to Mecca

c. criticizes *It's a Wise Child*, the radio quiz show that had featured all of the Glass children

d. boasts to her parents, a one-time tap-dancing act, that she'll be more famous than they ever were

34. What was Spy vs. Spy?
a. John le Carré's first novel
b. a TV show whose main character was Maxwell Smart
c. the Ian Fleming novel that JFK made famous when he was photographed reading it in Palm Beach
d. a comic strip that ran in *Mad* magazine

35. Which distinguished American poet declined an invitation to the Johnson White House in protest over the Vietnam War?
a. Robert Frost
b. Allen Ginsberg
c. Robert Lowell
d. Sylvia Plath

36. *The Spy Who Came In from the Cold* was set in:
a. Siberia
b. London
c. Berlin
d. Washington

37. Two books by one author bracketed the decade. Name them.
a. *Breakfast at Tiffany's* and *In Cold Blood*, by Truman Capote
b. *The Electric Kool-Aid Acid Test* and *From Bauhaus to Our House*, by Tom Wolfe
c. *Myra Breckinridge* and *Lincoln*, by Gore Vidal
d. *Armies of the Night* and *Tough Guys Don't Dance*, by Norman Mailer

38. *Dispatches* was a collection of Michael Herr's journalism. What was it about?
a. the counterculture in San Francisco
b. the Soviet invasion of Czechoslovakia
c. the rock revolution
d. the war in Vietnam

39. Who wrote *The Best & the Brightest?*

a. David Susskind
b. David Horowitz
c. David Halberstam
d. David Harris

40. Who was Marvin the Torch?
a. the Chicago mafioso Studs Terkel made famous
b. one of Jimmy Breslin's fictional characters
c. a Miami arsonist
d. the subject of one of Art Buchwald's most brilliant columns

41. In the sixties, Dr. Hunter S. Thompson was:
a. a political writer for *Rolling Stone*
b. the president of the Medill school of journalism
c. the author of *Baby and Child Care*
d. a controversial medical columnist for *The Boston Phoenix*

42. Jann S. Wenner:
a. founded *The Village Voice* in New York
b. founded *City Magazine* in San Francisco
c. founded *The Boston Phoenix*
d. founded *Rolling Stone* in San Francisco

43. "Is _____ Dead?" was the cover line on a sixties issue of *Time*. Who did it refer to?
a. Paul McCartney
b. Eric Clapton
c. Bishop James Pike
d. God

44. *Our Bodies, Ourselves* was:
a. a women's health book
b. a feminist medical column syndicated in leading newspapers
c. a feminist look at funerals
d. the first Jane Fonda workout book

45. *The American Way of Death* was:
a. a novel set in the Southwest
b. the nonfiction book about the Sharon Tate murder
c. an investigation into the mortuary industry
d. a nonfiction book about the Hemlock Society

46. The title of Yoko Ono's sixties book was:

a. *Apple*
b. *Lemon*
c. *Orange*
d. *Grapefruit*

47. February 27, 1968, was the date of a memorable news report by Walter Cronkite. What did he say?

a. He wholeheartedly endorsed LBJ's policy in Vietnam.
b. He called for a negotiated settlement of the war.
c. He called Johnson a war criminal and demanded an immediate, unconditional surrender of all U.S. forces.
d. He called for the resignation of Ho Chi Minh.

Movies

1. The first film starring Jane Fonda and Robert Redford was:
a. *Barefoot in the Park*
b. *The Candidate*
c. *The Electric Horseman*
d. *The Chase*

2. After Bonnie and Clyde rob a bank, they hide out in the movies. The song they hear there is:
a. "Brother, Can You Spare a Dime?"
b. "Ain't Misbehavin'"
c. "Paper Moon"
d. "We're in the Money"

3. Their accomplice, whom the newspapers always described as an "unidentified suspect," was:
a. C.W. Post
b. C.W. Moss
c. John Wesley Harding
d. Virgil Starkweather

4. In *Cool Hand Luke*, Luke was played by:
a. Lee Marvin
b. Robert Redford
c. Steve McQueen
d. Paul Newman

5. In *Easy Rider*, Peter Fonda, Dennis Hopper, and Jack Nicholson sit around the campfire one night. Fonda turns Nicholson on to grass. They discuss:
a. the reason grass is better than booze
b. UFOs
c. the reason police hate men with long hair
d. Mardi Gras

6. In *Easy Rider*, just before Jack Nicholson is killed, he tells Dennis Hopper and Peter Fonda the reasons locals fear their long hair. It represents:
a. homosexuality
b. dirt
c. the Vietcong
d. freedom

7. "You know...we blew it" is the climax of:
a. *The Graduate*
b. *The Hustler*
c. *Easy Rider*
d. *North Dallas Forty*

8. Who played Mrs. Robinson in *The Graduate*?
a. Jean Stapleton
b. Anne Bancroft
c. Shelley Winters
d. Estelle Getty

9. In *The Graduate*, where was Benjamin when he was advised to go into plastics?
a. in bed with Mrs. Robinson
b. poolside, at a party at his family's home
c. in the lobby of the hotel before he reserved a room for his tryst with Mrs. Robinson
d. at the airport when he came home from college

10. In the last scene of *The Graduate*, how did Benjamin make sure no one would catch him and Elaine?
a. He removed the cross from the altar and barred the church door with it.

b. He jammed a ladder against the door he and Elaine made their escape through.

c. He and Elaine jumped on a bus to escape her parents, who had locked his car doors.

d. He sprayed tear gas at the crowd assembled for the wedding.

11. In *A Hard Day's Night*, Paul's grandfather is referred to as:

a. a short old man

b. a fat old man

c. a bald old man

d. a clean old man

12. When Paul's grandfather was taken to the police station at the end of *A Hard Day's Night*, he was:

a. getting married in the morning

b. with a group of his IRA friends, agitating against the police at Hyde Park

c. smuggling a woman his age up to his hotel room

d. selling pictures of the Beatles to their fans

13. What is John Lennon's answer in *A Hard Day's Night* when he is asked, "How did you find America?"

a. "I didn't. It found me."

b. "Great. We're more popular than Jesus there."

c. "Easy. Turn right after Greenland."

d. "America? What's America?"

14. When Jean-Paul Belmondo meets Jean Seberg in *Breathless*, she is:

a. reading *Under Milkwood*

b. selling the Paris edition of *The Herald Tribune*

c. in a café, after a film try-out with Otto Preminger

d. buying tickets to *The Harder They Fall*, a Bogart movie

15. In what movie does a character say, "Funny, you don't look blueish"?

a. *Blazing Saddles*

b. *Yellow Submarine*

c. *The Blues Brothers*

d. *The Attack of the Killer Tomatoes*

16. *The Battle of Algiers* influenced thousands of radicals. At demonstrations they often made a sound they heard in the movie. What was the sound:
a. shrieking
b. singing
c. keening
d. ululation

17. Who or what was the Pink Panther?
a. the cartoon character that dances around the opening credits of the movie
b. the name of the jewel that plays a major part in the movie
c. the nickname given to Inspector Clouseau
d. the name of the hotel where some of the movie's action takes place

18. In Antonioni's *Blow Up*, the photograph that is repeatedly blown up is of:
a. the woman that the star is in love with
b. a London orgy he has witnessed
c. a body in the park
d. a spy hidden in the woods

19. Paul Newman made his directional debut with which film:
a. *Sometimes a Great Notion*
b. *Ordinary People*
c. *Rachel, Rachel*
d. *The Sting*

20. Ciao! Manhattan was:
a. a gimmick invented by New York City theater-owners to get people to go to the movies
b. Clint Eastwood's first attempt at a spaghetti western
c. a favorite song in Bobby Short's repertoire at the Carlyle Hotel in New York; it became standard Muzak in movie theaters all over the country
d. an Andy Warhol movie starring Edie Sedgwick

21. The movie *Joe* was:
a. a knock-off of *Porgy and Bess*—a love story involving a crippled white ex-boxer and a Cuban shopkeeper in rundown Newark

b. the rock opera the Dave Clark Five wrote to capitalize on *Tommy*'s success

c. the bitter story of an angry member of the white working class, who rages at blacks and hippies

d. a lighthearted movie about a group of NYU graduate students who rob Fifth Avenue stores, all using the name Joe

22. Ratso Rizzo is a character in:

a. *Lonesome Cowboy*

b. *The Last Picture Show*

c. *Midnight Cowboy*

d. *The Dirty Dozen*

23. The name of Woody Allen's character in *Take the Money and Run* is:

a. Virgil Starkweather

b. Virgil Starkwell

c. Virgil Kane

d. Virgil Upton

24. Pussy Galore is a character in:

a. *Dr. Strangelove*

b. *From Russia With Love*

c. *Goldfinger*

d. *Dr. No*

25. In what movie did the sixties youth culture get the voting age reduced to fourteen, elect a republican rock singer President, put all people over thirty in concentration camps and feed them LSD?

a. *Wild in the Streets*

b. *Who's That Knockin' at My Door?*

c. *Steal This Book*

d. *Scorpio Rising*

26. *Petulia* was:

a. a movie about a British pop singer

b. a flower—a cross between a petunia and a tulip—developed by a Hollywood mogul

c. a British pop singer and composer who wrote soundtracks for several British films of the sixties

d. a film about a socialite and a surgeon

27. In *The Manchurian Candidate* Raymond Shaw, the protagonist, was "brainwashed" by:

a. his mother
b. a Hollywood film
c. creatures from outer space
d. Russian and Chinese doctors

28. The programming agent was:

a. his mother
b. a Hollywood film
c. creatures from outer space
d. a Russian doctor

29. The movie was withdrawn from circulation because:

a. Communists destroyed all the prints.
b. The sex scenes were too suggestive.
c. Frank Sinatra, the star, claimed it would promote violence in the wake of the assassination of President Kennedy.
d. The Russians and Koreans threatened to sue for defamation of national character.

30. In 1965, _____ won the Academy Award as the star of *Cat Ballou*.

a. Lee Marvin
b. Jane Fonda
c. Patricia Neal
d. Jack Lemmon

31. In *Rosemary's Baby*, Rosemary is tormented by:

a. self-doubts
b. guilt about her past
c. a coven of devil-worshipping witches
d. the fantasy that her apartment building is haunted

32. When she was pregnant, she had a craving for:

a. tanna root tea
b. raw meat
c. sex
d. visits with her friend Hutch

33. "Springtime for Hitler" is part of which movie:

a. *Day of the Locust*

b. *The Producers*
c. *The V.I.P.'s*
d. *Dr. Strangelove*

34. In the movie *Midnight Cowboy*, Joe Buck winds up hustling on 42nd Street. What was he before?
a. an investment broker
b. a drug dealer
c. a gigolo
d. an advertising executive

35. What scene, which had no nudity, was heralded as the sexiest of the decade?
a. the scene in *Bonnie and Clyde* where Bonnie finally succeeds in seducing Clyde
b. the death scene in *Romeo and Juliet*
c. the eating scene in *Tom Jones*
d. the last scene in *Last Tango in Paris*

36. What low-budget horror movie, directed by George Romero, became an instant cult classic?
a. *The Rocky Horror Picture Show*
b. *Night of the Living Dead*
c. *The Little Shop of Horrors*
d. *What Ever Happened to Baby Jane?*

37. What "art" film was initially banned in many cities but, when opened by court order, had lines around the block?
a. *Behind the Green Door*
b. *Deep Throat*
c. *I Am Curious (Yellow)*
d. *Emmanuelle*

38. Fellini's classic *8½* stars Marcello Mastroianni as:
a. a clown
b. Mussolini
c. the filmmaker
d. the Roman Emperor Nero

39. Antoine Doinel grew up in the sixties. Who was he?
a. François Truffaut's character who first appeared in *The 400 Blows* and appeared again in *Stolen Kisses*

b. a bumbling French police inspector played by Peter Sellers in the Pink Panther movies

c. a student-radical-turned-movie-star who first attracted attention on the barricades in Paris, 1968

d. a French film director who went out with Brigitte Bardot and Catherine Deneuve

40. Match the movie with the star:

a. *The Loneliness of the Long Distance Runner*	**1.** Vanessa Redgrave
b. *Darling*	**2.** Tom Courtenay
c. *Alfie*	**3.** Lynn Redgrave
d. *Morgan!*	**4.** Malcolm McDowell
e. *Georgy Girl*	**5.** Michael Caine
f. *Tom Jones*	**6.** Julie Christie
g. *If...*	**7.** Albert Finney
h. *Beckett*	**8.** Alan Bates
i. *Lawrence of Arabia*	**9.** Richard Burton
j. *King of Hearts*	**10.** Paul Scofield
k. *A Man for All Seasons*	**11.** Peter O'Toole

41. Complete the title of the movie: *Who's Afraid of _____?*
a. The Big Bad Wolf
b. Santa Claus
c. Elizabeth Taylor
d. Virginia Woolf

42. Fran Kubelik is a character in:
a. *The Sterile Cuckoo*
b. *The Apartment*
c. *Barefoot in the Park*
d. *The Pawnbroker*

43. "I wish for once you'd get here on time" is a line from *Butch Cassidy and the Sundance Kid.* Who says it and when?
a. Butch says it to Sundance when Sundance blows their first chance to escape.
b. Etta says it to Sundance as she seduces him.
c. Sheriff Bledsoe says it to Butch after staking out the bank he's heard Butch and Sundance are planning to rob.

d. Sundance says it to Etta, because she's kept him waiting, blowing their first escape attempt.

44. "I love you, Alice B. Toklas" is a line from the movie of the same name. Who says it and why?
a. Harold, played by Peter Sellers, says it to Alice as he tries to make Nancy jealous.
b. Harold says it to his mother, Alice B. Toklas, on her birthday.
c. Harold says it after eating some hash brownies.
d. Harold's father says it, trying to seduce Harold's girlfriend.

45. The young lovers in *Splendor in the Grass* are:
a. Warren Beatty and Natalie Wood
b. Richard Beymer and Natalie Wood
c. Warren Beatty and Julie Christie
d. Paul Newman and Natalie Wood

46. What's it all about _____?
a. Billy
b. Allie
c. Willie
d. Alfie

47. *Days of Wine and Roses* was a film about:
a. drug addiction
b. alcoholism
c. a mental institution
d. a women's prison

48. Fast Eddie is a character in:
a. *Cool Hand Luke*
b. *Hud*
c. *Bullitt*
d. *The Hustler*

Sports

1. A World Series catch transformed the 1969 Mets from underdogs to the Miracle Mets. Who hit the ball?
a. Brooks Robinson
b. Frank Robinson
c. Boog Powell
d. Willie Mays

2. Who caught it?
a. Ron Swoboda
b. Cleon Jones
c. Tommie Agee
d. Marv Throneberry

3. Who hit the home run over left field to win the 1960 World Series?
a. Bill Mazeroski
b. Mickey Mantle
c. Yogi Berra
d. Hank Smith

4. In 1968 who was the first thirty-game winner in the major leagues since Dizzy Dean in 1934?
a. Bob Gibson
b. Tom Seaver
c. Denny McLain
d. Mickey Lolich

5. Which team had a 6½ game lead in the National League on September 10, 1964, and then lost the pennant?
a. the Giants
b. the Phillies
c. the Cardinals
d. the Pirates

6. Sandy Koufax retired from the Los Angeles Dodgers in 1966 because:
a. He wanted to be a sports announcer.
b. He had arthritis in his left elbow.
c. He felt he was too old to pitch up to his standards.
d. He wanted to found his own computer company.

7. Which one of these contenders for the heavyweight title did not lose to Muhammad Ali?
a. George Chuvalo
b. Pete Redemacher
c. Zora Foley
d. Ernie Terrell

8. Where were the 1968 Winter Olympics held?
a. Sun Valley, U.S.A.
b. Innsbruck, Austria
c. Sapporo, Japan
d. Grenoble, France

9. In 1966, who set a world record by running a mile in 3:51.3, and then broke his own record with a time of 3:51.1 the next year?
a. Marty Liquori
b. Jim Ryun
c. Dyrol Burleson
d. Tom O'Hara

10. In 1969 the New York Mets, the New York Jets, and the New York Knicks all won championships. Their opponents were all teams from the same city. Which city?
a. Boston
b. Los Angeles
c. Baltimore
d. Detroit

11. Who said, "Can't anybody play this game"?

a. Tip O'Neill. He said it over a live microphone at the Red Sox game, but he was talking about the Democratic Party's fratricidal fight in 1968.

b. Willis Reed. He was furious about his teammates' performance in the championships in 1967.

c. Casey Stengel. He was talking about the 1962 Mets.

d. Boston Red Sox manager Dick Williams. He was trying to coax a win out of his team in the seventh game of the 1967 World Series.

12. In 1962, Mets' first baseman Marvelous Marv Throneberry hit a triple. He was called out for failing to touch first base. He would have been out anyway. Why?

a. He didn't touch third.

b. He didn't touch second.

c. He ran to third base first.

d. The third baseman tagged him while he was listening to manager Casey Stengel wrangle with the umpire.

13. Who pitched a three-hit shutout on two days of rest in the second game of the 1965 World Series?

a. Bob Gibson

b. Whitey Ford

c. Sandy Koufax

d. Don Drysdale

14. The "Doomsday Defense" was:

a. a nickname for the Green Bay Packers' defense

b. a vision concocted by nuclear futurologist Herman Kahn

c. a nickname for the Dallas Cowboys' defense

d. the Russians' ultimate weapon in *Dr. Strangelove*

15. Yaz had his best year in 1967. Can you describe his value to the Red Sox?

a. He was rookie of the year.

b. He was the highest paid member of the team.

c. He won baseball's triple crown.

d. He was soon to become a league executive and players looked to him to represent their interests.

16. Who said, "Winning isn't everything; it's the only thing."
a. Joseph Kennedy, talking about why he'd taught his children to excel in sports
b. Vince Lombardi
c. Tom Landry
d. Richard Nixon, talking about football

17. Roger Maris hit sixty-one home runs in
a. 1960
b. 1961
c. 1962
d. 1963

18. He broke Babe Ruth's record. Why did some say his feat should have an asterisk in the record books?
a. because the season was longer by eight games
b. because the season was longer by ten games
c. because the season was longer by five games
d. none of the above

19. In 1968 who was the most acclaimed pitcher in the major leagues when he won 31 games?
a. Tom Seaver
b. Sandy Koufax
c. Denny McLain
d. Juan Marichal

20. Name the three centers who dominated professional basketball in the late sixties.
a. Dave Cowens, Wilt Chamberlain, Nate Thurmond
b. Wilt Chamberlain, Bill Russell, Nate Thurmond
c. Nate Thurmond, Dave Cowens, Bill Russell
d. none of the above

21. Who was the first man to shatter a backboard on a dunk?
a. Lew Alcindor
b. Wilt Chamberlain
c. Bill Russell
d. Chuck Conners

22. In *Ball Four* Jim Bouton wrote about a "beaver shoot." It was:

a. the term Mickey Mantle and Whitey Ford used when they eyeballed women on the road

b. the phrase Bouton used for the hunting trips he and his teammates took during off days

c. his fastball

d. the closing days of the 1966 pennant race

23. Paul Hornung was suspended from the NFL for:
a. flashing
b. womanizing
c. gambling
d. cheating

24. Vince Lombardi's 1967 Green Bay Packers defeated _____ for their record-breaking third straight National Football League championship:
a. the Los Angeles Rams
b. the San Francisco Giants
c. the Chicago Bears
d. the Dallas Cowboys

25. They won the game:
a. in the first period when quarterback Zeke Bratkowski, who was replacing an ailing Bart Starr, passed to Boyd Dowler for three straight touchdowns
b. in the middle of the fourth period, when Don Chandler connected for three straight field goals
c. with three seconds to go in the fourth period, when Bart Starr leapt into the end zone after guard Jerry Kramer had blocked Jethro Pugh
d. in the second overtime, when Travis Williams made a ninety-five-yard kickoff return

26. Who gave the black power salute at the 1968 Olympics?
a. John Carlos
b. Harry Edwards
c. Tommie Smith
d. Moses Malone

27. Who said, "Save your money and don't bet on Sonny"?
a. Little Richard, about Sonny and Cher

b. Paul Hornung, about Sonny Jergensen

c. Muhammad Ali, about Sonny Liston

d. Willie Shoemaker, about Sunny Jim Fitzsimmons

28. Who pitched no-hitters in 1962, 1963, 1964, and 1965?
a. Bob Gibson
b. Don Drysdale
c. Jim Palmer
d. Sandy Koufax

29. Match the fighter with Muhammad Ali's nickname for him:

a. Ernie Terrell	**1.** the Ugly Bear
b. Sonny Liston	**2.** the Washerwoman
c. Floyd Patterson	**3.** the Octopus
d. George Chuvalo	**4.** the Rabbit

30. Which pitcher did not pitch in a World Series because of religious reasons?
a. Bo Belinsky
b. Mickey Lolich
c. Denny McLain
d. Sandy Koufax

31. Abebe Bikila won the marathon in the Rome Olympics. His win was memorable because:
a. He collapsed and was rushed to the hospital immediately after his win.
b. His time has never been beaten.
c. He ran without shoes.
d. none of the above

32. He was also at the 1968 Olympics. What happened to him there?
a. He led a demonstration against white imperialists.
b. Once again, he was a competitor. He placed third.
c. He was a government minister. As a representative of his country, he denounced U.S. involvement in Vietnam.
d. He entered the marathon but had to drop out when he suffered a bone fracture. The following year, an automobile accident left him paralyzed and confined to a wheelchair.

TV and Radio

1. The TV show that first brought Bill Cosby to national attention was
a. *I Spy*
b. *Get Smart*
c. *Fat Albert*
d. *The Tonight Show* with Johnny Carson

2. In 1968 the character on the Smothers Brothers show who ran for President was:
a. Dick Smothers
b. Tom Smothers
c. Pat Paulsen
d. Steve Martin

3. Murray the K was:
a. a radio announcer impresario who dubbed himself the Fifth Beatle when the Fab Four came to New York in 1964
b. the name Jason Robards' ward in *A Thousand Clowns* chose for himself in a TV production
c. the first host of a phone-in radio show
d. a late-night radio personality who broadcast from Mexico

4. Jacqueline Kennedy hosted a TV show on:
a. a tour of the White House
b. alcoholism and drug addiction

c. Picasso's artistic career

d. the plight of the homeless sleeping outside the White House

5. In the sixties Ryan O'Neal came to public attention as:

a. one of the Monkees

b. a star of *Peyton Place*

c. one of two American actors who was a TV star in France

d. a reader of *Finnegan's Wake* in an ongoing radio production

6. Wolfman Jack was:

a. a disc jockey at the discotheque Arthur

b. the founder of WBAI, listener-sponsored radio in New York

c. a bizarre radio personality who broadcast from Mexico

d. the host of the afternoon horror-movie show that replaced *American Bandstand* in the hearts of America's teenagers

7. Which TV character on which TV show was known for sitting near what famous piece of sculpture?

a. Harriet Nelson, on *The Adventures of Ozzie and Harriet,* in front of the *Pieta*

b. Sergeant Chip Saunders on *Combat,* in front of the Iwo Jima statue

c. Dobie Gillis, next to *The Thinker,* on *The Many Loves of Dobie Gillis*

d. Constance Mackenzie, on *Peyton Place,* in front of the Minuteman statue in Concord, Massachusetts

8. Which TV show featured the Champagne Lady?

a. *The Ed Sullivan Show*

b. *Gunsmoke*

c. *The Lawrence Welk Show*

d. *The Tonight Show*

9. Which celebrity's habit of constantly combing his hair on his TV show led to a hit record? What show was he associated with?

a. Fabian, a teen idol who was introduced on *American Bandstand*

b. Actor Edd Byrnes, who played the character Kookie on *77 Sunset Strip*

c. Peter Tork, of *The Monkees*

d. Rick Nelson, on *The Adventures of Ozzie and Harriet*

10. Who ran the Longbranch Saloon on Gunsmoke?
a. Chester
b. Festus
c. Ma Smalley
d. Kitty Russell

11. What were Beaver's parents names on *Leave It to Beaver*?
a. Ozzie and Harriet
b. Alex and Donna
c. Ward and June
d. Jim and Margaret

12. Who was Sergeant Schultz?
a. the main character in *No Time for Sergeants*
b. the guard of Stalag 13 on *Hogan's Heroes*
c. the army liaison officer on *McHale's Navy*
d. the main character on *Combat*

13. Who refused to appear on *Hootenany* and why?
a. the Limelighters, because they said the show was too controversial
b. Phil Ochs, because he said the fee he was offered was too low
c. Joan Baez, because, it was said, the program had blacklisted other performers
d. the Smothers Brothers, because they objected to network censorship

14. Name the original three sons on *My Three Sons*
a. Steve, Robbie, and Mike Douglas
b. Bub, Robbie, and Chip Douglas
c. Mike, Robbie, and Chip Douglas
d. Sudsy, Bub, and Steve Douglas

15. What was the name of the hospital on *Dr. Kildare*?
a. St. Elizabeth's
b. County General
c. Blair General
d. Belleview

16. What was the name of Ben Casey's original mentor on Ben Casey?

a. Dr. Leonard Gillespie
b. Dr. Marcus Welby
c. Dr. David Zorba
d. Dr. Benjamin Franklin Pierce

17. What was the name of the boat on *McHale's Navy?*
a. P.T. 109
b. P.T. 73
c. *The Taratupa*
d. *Old Lead Bottom*

18. Buz and Tod drove along _____:
a. Route 66
b. Sunset Strip
c. the Pacific Coast Highway
d. the Hollywood Freeway

19. Jonathan Steed was the main character of:
a. *The Avengers*
b. *The Man From U.N.C.L.E.*
c. *I Spy*
d. *Hawaii Five-O*

20. The Lennon Sisters were:
a. John Lennon's half-sisters, who formed an acrobatic act that performed regularly on *The Ed Sullivan Show*
b. a singing group that appeared on *The Lawrence Welk Show*
c. an early Motown group, the first to appear on *The Ed Sullivan Show*
d. a troupe of dancers who spun off from the June Taylor Dancers and got their first big break on Jackie Gleason's variety show

21. The Smothers Brothers program was cancelled when:
a. Tommy told a joke making fun of Richard Nixon.
b. Dick pretended to light up a joint, and passed it to some stagehands.
c. Tommy and Dick allowed a segment sarcastic of religion to appear.
d. Tommy and Dick insisted on letting Pete Seeger sing "Knee Deep in the Big Muddy."

22. Who was the Great One?
a. Dean Martin
b. Danny Thomas
c. Jackie Gleason
d. Lawrence Welk

23. Tiny Tim and his wife Miss Vicki were married:
a. in the Abyssinian Baptist Church
b. on *The Tonight Show*
c. onstage at Radio City Music Hall
d. in a tulip garden in New York's Central Park

24. David McCallum starred in
a. *I Spy*
b. *The Man from U.N.C.L.E.*
c. *Get Smart*
d. *Batman*

25. *Julia* was:
a. a ground-breaking show about a black nurse
b. a novel by Gore Vidal, long talked-about as a future TV project
c. a made-for-TV movie, written by John Lennon and dedicated to his mother's memory
d. a made-for-TV movie about Lillian Hellman

26. Who said, "Television is a vast wasteland"?
a. T.S. Eliot, on a visit to America
b. Jackie Gleason, when he cancelled his game show *You're in the Picture* after just one week
c. FCC chairman Newton Minow, in a speech to broadcasters
d. George C. Scott, when *East Side, West Side* became one of the few quality shows to win a large audience

27. One of Beaver's pals on *Leave It to Beaver* was:
a. Lumpy
b. Gilbert
c. Wally
d. Bub

28. "Here come de judge" was:
a. a routine on *Rowan & Martin's Laugh-In*

b. The call that traditionally began court sessions in Washington, D.C. After a report on a local news program, civil rights activists protested, calling it racist and it was discontinued.

c. J.J.'s fond greeting for his father on *Good Times*

d. a sarcastic remark made by Supreme Court Justice Abe Fortas and picked up by an open mike during a Senate hearing

29. The phrase "Would you believe" became popular after:

a. Spiro Agnew used it as a litany for an anti-media speech.

b. Tug McGraw, interviewed live, exulted over the 1969 Miracle Mets victories.

c. Howard Cosell exclaimed it during boxing matches and football games.

d. Maxwell Smart used it on the show *Get Smart.*

30. The "Flying Fickle Finger of Fate" was:

a. the award given by Secretary of Health, Education, and Welfare Anthony Celebrezze to the business "goon of the month"

b. a running gag in the TV show Get Smart

c. the euphemism used by sportscasters when an American athlete gave a Soviet athlete the finger during the 1964 Olympics

d. a weekly routine on *Rowan & Martin's Laugh-In*

31. Who was *That Girl?*

a. Mary Tyler Moore

b. Marlo Thomas

c. Valerie Harper

d. Jane Curtin

32. On what program did talk-show host David Frost make his American debut?

a. as a fill-in for Johnny Carson on *The Tonight Show*

b. as the host of *That Was the Week That Was*

c. as the host of *60 Minutes*

d. as a fill-in for David Susskind on *The David Susskind Show*

33. Eddie was one of Wally's friends on *Leave It to Beaver.* His last name was:

a. Anderson

b. Stone

c. Cleaver

d. Haskell

34. "And that's the way it is" was the sign-off for:

a. Chet Huntley and David Brinkley

b. Howard K. Smith

c. John Chancellor

d. Walter Cronkite

35. Which of the following was *not* a part of the TV series *Batman*:

a. The Boy Wonder

b. The Caped Crusader

c. The Dynamic Duo

d. Kato

36. Gomer Pyle lived in:

a. Mayview

b. Mayville

c. Mayburg

d. Mayberry

37. Jed Clampett was the main character on:

a. *The Beverly Hillbillies*

b. *Petticoat Junction*

c. *Hee Haw*

d. *Hootenany*

38. Barney Fife was a regular character on:

a. *McHale's Navy*

b. *The Andy Griffith Show*

c. *Gomer Pyle, U.S.M.C.*

d. *The Beverly Hillbillies*

39. *American Bandstand* was originally filmed in:

a. New York

b. Los Angeles

c. Detroit

d. Philadelphia

40. Pete and Julie were two members of *The Mod Squad*. Who was the third?

a. Lonnie

b. Lenny
c. Linc
d. Les

41. What show did Captain Parmenter appear on?
a. *Hogan's Heroes*
b. *McHale's Navy*
c. *Combat*
d. *F Troop*

42. James Garner played:
a. Bart Maverick
b. Beau Maverick
c. Brent Maverick
d. Bret Maverick

43. Napoleon Solo was a character on:
a. *I Spy*
b. *The Man From U.N.C.L.E.*
c. *Get Smart*
d. *The Avengers*

44. *Dragnet* was located in:
a. Chicago
b. San Diego
c. Miami
d. Los Angeles

45. Wilma was married to:
a. Barney
b. Fred
c. Norton
d. Jed

46. Their neighbors were:
a. Barney and Betty
b. Pebbles and Bamm Bamm
c. Norton and Trixie
d. Ward and June

47. "You bet your bippy" was a line from:
a. *The Jackie Gleason Show*

b. *I Spy*
c. *Rowan & Martin's Laugh-In*
d. *Batman*

48. Match the cops with the shows:

a. Sergeant Joe Friday	**1.** *Naked City*
b. Eliot Ness	**2.** *Dragnet*
c. Detective Adam Flint	**3.** *The F.B.I.*
d. Officer Francis Muldoon	**4.** *The Untouchables*
e. Inspector Lewis Erskine	**5.** *Car 54, Where Are You?*

49. Wilbur Post had:
a. a pet dolphin, Flipper
b. a mother who was a car
c. a pet bear named Gentle Ben
d. a talking horse named Mr. Ed

50. Allen Ludden was the host of:
a. *Queen for a Day*
b. *Jeopardy*
c. *Password*
d. *The Price Is Right*

Pop Culture

1. Peter Max was:
a. a sixties artist
b. Jacqueline Kennedy's hairdresser
c. Andy Warhol's favorite filmmaker
d. a T-shirt manufacturer who invented the process of tie-dying

2. In the mid sixties Betsey Johnson designed clothes for the fashionable store:
a. Raffles
b. Paraphernalia
c. Scruples
d. Betsey, Bunkie & Nini

3. If you were at a chic party in 1968 and saw women wearing white boots you'd assume they were:
a. early feminists who regarded Nancy Sinatra's "These Boots Are Made for Walkin'" as their anthem.
b. hookers
c. customers at Courreges
d. Chicago White Sox fans

4. In 1967, Mia Farrow was married to:
a. Woody Allen
b. André Previn
c. Frank Sinatra
d. the Maharishi Mahesh Yogi

5. The Freedom Seder was
a. a ballet by Merce Cunningham
b. a demonstration by the Jewish Defense League during Passover of 1968 designed to show that the sixties Jew was no longer assimilated, but was militant and free
c. a "liberation seder," written by the political activist Arthur Waskow, which superimposed modern left-wing politics on the traditional Haggadah
d. a novel by Elie Wiesel

6. Penelope Tree was:
a. a wilderness campsite in western Massachusetts where a group of long-haired activists established the commune Omega
b. the musky cologne that gave many beaded, tie-dyed hippies their special scent
c. a slim blonde model
d. a soft-rock song that rose to the top of the Billboard charts just as "Winchester Cathedral" was falling

7. Name the scents: English _____ for women; English _____ for men.
a. Lilac, for women; Tweed, for men
b. Lace, for women; Spice, for men
c. Lavender, for women; Leather, for men
d. Patchover, for women; Musk for men

8. Blue Cheer was:
a. a Beach Boys hit
b. an Elvis Presley movie
c. a Hawaiian minor league baseball team
d. one of Owsley's most popular brands of LSD

9. The Daughters of Bilitis was:
a. a short-lived TV show—a feminist response to *Star Trek*
b. an early lesbian organization
c. a group of daughters of mothers with eating disorders
d. a society of mushroom aficionados

10. Summerhill was:
a. a brand of mentholated cigarettes
b. a ballet by George Balanchine

c. a school—and later a book—whose premise was that children learn best with permissive education

d. a community in Costa Rica, founded by Quakers, which became a mecca for hippies

11. Who asked, "Is it true blondes have more fun"?
a. Marilyn Monroe
b. Clairol ads
c. publicists for the Miss Rheingold contest
d. an ad for *Gentlemen Prefer Blondes*

12. To "grok" was to:
a. search for the most tantalizing undefined particle in physics
b. blow up a hut suspected of hiding enemy Vietcong
c. take a breather during a hike and eat a trail treat—raisins, nuts, and M&Ms
d. to absorb, imbibe, embody sensations or information

13. The Wedge was
a. the formation on the defensive line that kept the Green Bay Packers at the top of the NFL
b. the DC Comics' superhero who was billed as the new Plasticman
c. a hair style invented by Vidal Sassoon
d. a style of women's shoes

14. DMT was:
a. a drug that gave a quick LSD-like hit
b. the region in Vietnam where the Hmong tribesmen lived
c. the Department of Military Transfers—a favorite target of the anti-war movement
d. a rock group—a spinoff from the Kinks

15. "The one beer to have when you're having more than one" was:
a. Budweiser
b. Schlitz
c. Pabst
d. Schaefer

16. What cigarette tasted good, "like a cigarette should"?
a. Winston

b. Lark
c. Marlboro
d. Kool

17. What soft drink was "wet and wild"?
a. Sprite
b. Royal Crown Cola
c. Mountain Dew
d. 7-Up

18. Who was Barbie's best friend?
a. Cynthia
b. Sally
c. Midge
d. Annie

19. Metrecal was:
a. a new form of poetic rhythm favored by the poets who frequented Lawrence Ferlinghetti's City Lights bookstore
b. a California health plan
c. Governor Ronald Reagan's plan for a new train system
d. a diet drink

20. Catholic women were scandalized by a photo taken of Jacqueline Kennedy on her way to Mass. What was she wearing?
a. Vacationing at Hyannis Port, she wore a madras wraparound skirt, a T-shirt, and sandals. The scandal was, she wasn't wearing a hat.
b. The problem was what she wasn't wearing—gloves.
c. She wore a mantilla instead of a hat and she was gloveless.
d. She was wearing jeans.

21. Kenneth was:
a. the computer in *2001*
b. Jacqueline Kennedy's milliner. He created the pillbox hat.
c. Jacqueline Kennedy's hairdresser
d. a star of kung fu movies

22. If you were a woman and took a comb and snarled your hair from back to front, you were:
a. teasing it

106

b. making your scalp more sensual
c. growing dreads, like the Rastafarians
d. getting rid of lice

23. Evelyn Wood was:
a. John F. Kennedy's secretary
b. a character on *Upstairs, Downstairs*
c. Richard Nixon's secretary
d. the founder of a speed reading school

24. During the late sixties, two foods and two fragrances became staples. What were they?
a. The foods were raspberry vinegar and Häagen-Dazs; the fragrances were Opium and Giorgio.
b. The foods were bran flakes and Trail Mix; the fragrances were musk oil and Canoe.
c. The foods were carrot juice and lemon grass; the fragrances were Rive Gauche and Eau Sauvage.
d. The foods were brown rice and granola; the fragrances were patchouli and sandalwood incense.

25. One designer came up with the topless bathing suit. Who was he/she?
a. Mary Quant
b. Betsey Johnson
c. Rudi Gernreich
d. Yves St. Laurent

26. The "in" disco in New York City was Arthur, run by Sybil Christopher. Her former husband was:
a. Eddie Fisher
b. John Lennon
c. Jason Epstein
d. Richard Burton

27. I Ching was:
a. the leader of the North Vietnamese forces
b. the leader of China's Cultural Revolution
c. a Chinese system of prophecy
d. the popular TV personality who hosted a Chinese cooking show

28. Paul Morrissey was:
a. a guard for the Boston Celtics
b. one of Robert Kennedy's closest advisors
c. one of Andy Warhol's closest advisors
d. Chicago's district attorney during the 1968 Democratic Convention

29. The "Gathering of the Tribes—the First Human Be-In" was held:
a. in Hyde Park, London
b. in Tompkins Square Park, New York
c. in Griffith Park, Los Angeles
d. in Golden Gate Park, San Francisco

30. The London street that stood for avant-garde fashion in the early sixties was:
a. Piccadilly
b. Carnaby
c. Bond
d. Kensington High Street

31. The Nehru jacket became popular in America:
a. after black leader Stokely Carmichael began to wear it as a sign that he had matured into a Third World leader
b. after the war between China and India
c. after the Maharaj Ji moved to America and instructed his adherents to show sympathy with India in a visible way
d. after the Beatles visited the Maharishi Mahesh Yogi in India

32. The first apartment complex built specifically for singles was in:
a. Miami, Florida
b. Torrance, California
c. Santa Monica, California
d. Phoenix, Arizona

33. Who was Carol Doda?
a. an exotic dancer romantically linked with JFK
b. a topless dancer well known for her silicon implants
c. Robert F. Kennedy's secretary
d. the inventor of the Hula Hoop

34. Of the many medical advances of the decade, one profoundly changed the way we live. What was it?

a. the development of the heart transplant

b. the discovery that cigarette smoking causes cancer

c. the discovery that cyclamates are carcinogens

d. the development of the Pill

THE ANSWERS

POLITICS AND NEWS

1.d; 2.b; 3.d; 4.b; 5.c; 6.a; 7.b; 8.c; 9.b; 10.c; 11.c; 12.b; 13.d; 14.d; 15.a; 16.c; 17.b; 18.c; 19.c; 20.d; 21.c; 22.b; 23.b; 24.c; 25.c; 26.d; 27.c; 28.a; 29.c; 30.c; 31.a; 32.c; 33.d; 34.c; 35.c; 36.d; 37.d; 38.a; 39.d; 40.b; 41.c; 42.d; 43.d; 44.b; 45.a; 46.a; 47.a; 48.d; 49.d; 50.a; 51.a; 52.c; 53.a; 54.b; 55.c; 56.b; 57.d; 58.b; 59.c; 60.b; 61.c; 62.b; 63.a; 64.c; 65.b; 66.c; 67.a-3, b-4, c-1, d-2; 68.a; 69.b; 70.a; 71.c; 72.d; 73.c; 74.a; 75.d; 76.c; 77.c; 78.b; 79.a; 80.c; 81.c; 82.b; 83.c; 84.a; 85.c; 86.b; 87.d; 88.d; 89.d; 90.c; 91.a; 92.a; 93.b; 94.c; 95.b; 96.c; 97.d; 98.a; 99.c; 100.d; 101.d; 102.a; 103.c; 104.c; 105.a; 106.c; 107.a; 108.d; 109.c; 110.b; 111.a; 112.c; 113.d; 114.d; 115.c; 116.a; 117.b; 118.b; 119.d; 120.b; 121.d; 122.c; 123.c; 124.b; 125.c; 126.b; 127.b; 128.c; 129.d; 130.c; 131.b; 132.c; 133.a-3, b-1, c-2, d-4; 134.c; 135.d; 136.b; 137.b; 138.b; 139.b; 140.b; 141.b; 142.b; 143.b; 144.d; 145.c; 146.b; 147.c; 148.b; 149.c; 150.d; 151.b; 152.c; 153.c; 154.d; 155.d; 156.a; 157.c; 158.b; 159.d; 160.d; 161.b; 162.b&c; 163.a-3, b-2, c-5, d-7, e-6, f-4, g-1; 164.c; 165.c; 166.b; 167.a&b; 168.a; 169.a; 170.c; 171.c&d; 172.b; 173.d; 174.c; 175.a; 176.b; 177.c; 178.c; 179.b; 180.a; 181.d; 182.d; 183.c; 184.b; 185.d; 186.c; 187.d; 188.b; 189.d.

MUSIC

1.b; 2.a; 3.a&d; 4.b; 5.c; 6.b&d; 7.a-1, b-2, c-3, d-4; 8.d; 9.d; 10.d;
11.c; 12.a; 13.d; 14.d; 15.c; 16.a; 17.a; 18.b; 19.c; 20.b; 21.d;
22.c; 23.d; 24.b; 25.c; 26.c; 27.d; 28.b; 29.b; 30.b; 31.a; 32.a;
33.b; 34.c; 35.c; 36.d; 37.b; 38.b; 39.c; 40.d; 41.b; 42.b; 43.b;
44.a; 45.a; 46.b; 47.c; 48.c; 49.a-2, b-4, c-1, d-3; 50.d; 51.b;
52.b; 53.b; 54.c; 55.c; 56.d; 57.a; 58.b; 59.d; 60.a-2, b-4, c-3,
d-1; 61.b; 62.a; 63.a; 64.b; 65.c; 66.c; 67.b; 68.d; 69.b; 70.c;
71.d; 72.b; 73.a; 74.a; 75.c; 76.b; 77.b; 78.c; 79.d; 80.d; 81.a;
82.c; 83.a; 84.b; 85.a; 86.d; 87.b; 88.c; 89.b; 90.c; 91.c; 92.b;
93.c; 94.a; 95.a; 96.d; 97.c; 98.d; 99.a; 100.d; 101.b; 102.d;
103.c; 104.d; 105.c; 106.c; 107.b; 108.d; 109.c; 110.c; 111.d;
112.c; 113.b; 114.c; 115.d; 116.a; 117.d; 118.d; 119.b; 120.a;
121.d; 122.d; 123.b; 124.c; 125.a; 126.c; 127.d; 128.c; 129.b;
130.b; 131.a; 132.b; 133.d; 134.b; 135.c; 136.b; 137.b; 138.b;
139.b; 140.d; 141.c; 142.d; 143.c; 144.a; 145.a-3, b-6, c-7, d-1,
e-2, f-5, g-4; 146.c; 147.b; 148.c; 149.d; 150.b; 151.b; 152.b;
153.d

THEATER

1.c; 2.b; 3.c; 4.d; 5.c; 6.d; 7.b; 8.c; 9.d; 10.b; 11.a&d; 12.c; 13.b;
14.b; 15.b; 16.d; 17.b; 18.c; 19.b; 20.c; 21.a; 22.c; 23.b; 24.c;
25.b; 26.d; 27.c; 28.c; 29.b

LITERATURE AND JOURNALISM

1.c; 2.b; 3.d; 4.b; 5.d; 6.a; 7.a; 8.b; 9.c; 10.b; 11.c; 12.a; 13.a-3,
b-5, c-4, d-1, e-2; 14.d; 15.b; 16.d; 17.c; 18.a; 19.b; 20.c; 21.b;
22.b; 23.d; 24.c; 25.d; 26.c; 27.c; 28.a; 29.b; 30.d; 31.a; 32.b;
33.a; 34.d; 35.c; 36.c; 37.a; 38.d; 39.c; 40.b; 41.a; 42.d; 43.d;
44.a; 45.c; 46.d; 47.b

MOVIES

1.d; 2.d; 3.b; 4.d; 5.b; 6.d; 7.c; 8.b; 9.b; 10.a; 11.d; 12.d; 13.c; 14.b; 15.b; 16.d; 17.a&b; 18.c; 19.c; 20.d; 21.c; 22.c; 23.b; 24.c; 25.a; 26.d; 27.d; 28.a; 29.c; 30.a; 31.a&c; 32.b; 33.b; 34.c; 35.c; 36.b; 37.c; 38.c; 39.a; 40.a-2, b-6, c-5, d-1, e-3, f-7, g-4, h-9, i&h-11, j&e-8, k-10; 41.d; 42.b; 43.b; 44.c; 45.a; 46.d; 47.b; 48.d

SPORTS

1.a; 2.a; 3.a; 4.c; 5.b; 6.b; 7.b; 8.d; 9.b; 10.c; 11.c; 12.b; 13.c; 14.c; 15.c; 16.b; 17.b; 18.a; 19.c; 20.b; 21.d; 22.a; 23.c; 24.d; 25.c; 26.a&c; 27.c; 28.d; 29.a-1, b-4, c-2, d-3; 30.d; 31.c; 32.d.

TV and RADIO

1.a; 2.c; 3.a; 4.a; 5.b; 6.c; 7.c; 8.c; 9.b; 10.d; 11.c; 12.b; 13.c; 14.c; 15.c; 16.c; 17.b; 18.a; 19.a; 20.b; 21.c&d; 22.c; 23.b; 24.b; 25.a; 26.c; 27.b; 28.a; 29.d; 30.d; 31.b; 32.b; 33.d; 34.d; 35.d; 36.d; 37.a; 38.b; 39.d; 40.c; 41.d; 42.d; 43.b; 44.d; 45.b; 46.a; 47.c; 48.a-2, b-4, c-1, d-5, e-3; 49.d; 50.c

POP CULTURE

1.a; 2.b; 3.c; 4.c; 5.c; 6.c; 7.c; 8.d; 9.b; 10.c; 11.b; 12.d; 13.c; 14.a; 15.d; 16.a; 17.d; 18.c; 19.d; 20.c; 21.c; 22.a; 23.d; 24.d; 25.c; 26.d; 27.c; 28.c; 29.d; 30.b; 31.d; 32.b; 33.b; 34.d